The Day The Musick Died

The Day The Musick Died

A Mother-Daughter Addiction Journey of
Suffering, Loss and a Ray of Hope

Cheryl Hughes Musick

ISBN: 1540856437
ISBN 13: 9781540856432
Library of Congress Control Number: 2016920353
CreateSpace Independent Publishing Platform
North Charleston, South Carolina

Author's Note

ALL OF THE events and experiences chronicled in this book are true and accurate, to the best of my recollection. I apologize for any inadvertent errors in recounting any of the specific details and timelines of this story.

Some of the names of people mentioned in the book have been changed, and some of their identifying circumstances altered, to preserve confidentiality and privacy.

The situations mentioned in this book may hit close to home for some readers. It is not meant to offend anyone, but to bring to light the hideous affects of substance abuse on addicts and their families. My intention in writing this book is to educate people to the dangers of addiction and bring light to the current heroin epidemic raging across our country stealing lives, and to offer resources and hope for recovery.

If you are a struggling addict or someone who is affected by addictions, I hope Misty's painfully candid story will inspire you to find help and hope for a bright and sober future.

Cheryl

Rob & Kelly — I want you to know how much your Brother Jim means to my Husband and I, as we know the Lord placed him on that freeway at that precise time for a reason. We are eternally grateful. Bless you all as a family —

Cheryl

Table of Contents

Introduction

THIS IS NOT the book that I *wanted* to write, but it's the book that I *need* to write.

You see, a few years ago I was expecting to share an inspirational story, a moving chronicle of courage and triumph. Told in alternating voices of mother and daughter, that book was going to capture how my beloved daughter Misty summoned the strength to follow the path of recovery from drug addiction and reclaim her life, and how I stood by her through all the trials and tribulations. We planned to unveil all the heartache, all the destructive choices, all the battles against the demons, and finally all the joys of a dark and difficult journey that ultimately led to a beautiful finish. Our hope was to serve as one uplifting reminder to addicts and their mothers, fathers and other loved ones that when you are caught in the vice-like grip of addiction it really is possible to break on through to the other side.

Sadly, the dream of that book, like so many dreams I clung to for Misty and our family, was smashed to pieces in a minivan on an interstate highway in Arizona early one summer morning in 2015. In her long, agonizing struggle with alcohol and drugs, Misty didn't make it.

However, while I didn't understand it at first, my mission to tell Misty's story did not end when my daughter took her last breath. I discovered that although I could no longer write the book that I had hoped and planned to write, there was another story just waiting to be told. The characters are the same—my daughter Misty and I waging our battle against the immense power of addiction. The purpose of bringing our story to light remains unchanged: to encourage and motivate addicts and their families to never give up, to reach out for help and support, to write a successful and triumphant ending to their own story. As strange as it may sound, I am just as passionate and hopeful about this opportunity to tell you all about Misty and me as I was a few years ago. Maybe I'm even *more* determined. You will soon learn why.

The seeds for this new mission were planted on Facebook, in those first days after tragedy rocked our family's world, when my son Brian courageously unveiled his raw feelings about what happened and what it meant to him.

> *"My sister, Misty Brooke Sanchez, died on 7/27/2015 in a fatal car accident. The reality and truth is that she died some time before that date.*
>
> *Misty was a hero to many, including myself. Everyone knew her talent and her insane motivation and drive. Misty inspired many with her charisma and super personality. Misty was my 2nd favorite female vocalist (2nd only to Amy Lee, one of her idols) and she was an amazing pianist. Misty was loving, caring, and a fun mother. She was a person who lacked fear and loved facing the impossible. She was the spirit of a wild horse never to be tamed, however....*
>
> *My sister was an addict.*
>
> *Misty spent the last 2 years battling hardcore drug and alcohol addiction. She spent a year and a half in county jail for committing many felonies. She had chance after chance to get her life back on track but she just kept falling back into the world of drugs. The last 3 weeks of her life were spent running from the law, living the life of an outlaw.*
>
> *I'm far beyond angry.*
>
> *Misty chose drugs over her family, her children and her friends. I can honestly say that we all did the very best that we could to help her and keep her on the right path. In the*

midst of all the love and support that she received she still made her choice and it was stupid and selfish.

I am the only one in my family who has not yet shed tears for Misty. I love her more than I can express, but I cannot comprehend how or why she could leave her own children the way she did. My rage is overshadowing my grief.

I want you all to know that I am not posting this to bash my sister at this horrible time. Let me make my real point:

If you are battling drug or alcohol addiction, PLEASE GET HELP!

Misty was one of the strongest people that I ever knew and even she was not strong enough to break the chains of drug addiction. If you knew Misty then you would know that if anyone could overcome drug addiction, it would definitely be my sister. But drugs will take a person and twist them into someone that you don't know. THAT was my sister these past 2 years; someone we no longer knew. She was but a shadow of her former self...the person we all loved. I can't count the number of people who are grieving right now because of losing her.

If you are caught in those chains of addiction, understand this: You cannot fight drug addiction on your own! PLEASE SEEK HELP! No one will think less of you for reaching out. There are some FREE places you can go to, for your own sake and for the sake of everyone who loves you.

Your life is precious, even if you do not believe it. You can overcome your addiction if you let people help you. There is no shame in admitting that you are not strong enough to break free on your own.

Please, don't let your loved ones go through what those who loved Misty are going through right now. Drugs just stole a person from our world who could have impacted MANY others in a powerful way. YOU are worth living...."

Did I cry reading Brian's powerful words? Absolutely, but then my house was flooded in tears during those first long, brutal days and nights after losing my precious first-born child, the girl I had loved and cared for since before she was born, the young woman with so many talents and gifts, the bubbly person with the power to light up any room the moment she walked into it. Then, amid my relentless sobbing, something else welled up. I felt proud of my son and grateful for his willingness to publicly expose his pain and anger. Brian has always had that ability to see things as they are and say what he believes needs to be said, no holding back. I learned that when he was a teenager and we had "debates" about his tastes in music!

I could totally understand Brian's feelings. There were countless moments when waves of anger would splash over my own deep pain and sadness. But I was trying with all my heart to learn to hate the *addiction* while still loving the addict—the *person* trapped in a pattern of terrifying, destructive, heart-breaking behavior. I don't believe Misty had "died" before that day when drugs ruled the stage and she lost her life amidst the broken meth pipes on a busy interstate outside Phoenix. I am convinced that even when addiction has taken over the thoughts, choices and actions of an addict, the individual is still present, somewhere beyond the clutches of this demonic possession.

Yes, my beloved Misty was still alive before the accident on that morning of July 27, 2015. And despite the terrible choices she had been making for far too long, I was still praying that she could finally turn in the right direction and save her life before it was too late.

I was re-reading Brian's post when he messaged me. "Mom, you won't believe what's happening!" he said. "I keep getting all these responses from my Facebook friends and strangers too. People are posting from Pennsylvania, New York, even Canada and England. I can hardly keep up with them all. Take a look!" I eagerly glanced through these follow-up messages:

"You made me cry, Brian. You reminded us that we all have just one life to live..."

"Brian, I can't shake the chills I got while reading your post. Your words hit home for me in so many ways..."

"Tears fill my eyes. I live a life similar to your sister's and my brother has not spoken to me in years and..."

"Thank you for sharing your heart. If this post can convince even one person to seek help it will be worth it..."

"From someone who has been in recovery for more than 30 years and who now works to help addicts today, I am pleased to tell you: WELL SAID."

"I am struggling with these same demons in my life right now and..."

As I dried my tears, a faint smile crept across my face. Brian sent a private message back to that last responder, encouraging her and reminding her where she could find help for her addiction...TODAY! My heart skipped a beat: my son may have just helped a struggling addict step onto the path to recovery. What a gift! The emotional responses from addicts and their loved ones kept pouring in, many bearing promises from addicts to seek help.

"You saved me," one addict wrote.

"I wake up and throughout the day re-read your message. I have never prayed so much or so hard or cried so much," revealed another.

Family members proclaimed a commitment to keep striving, to go on doing whatever they possibly could do to pull the addict in their lives back from the abyss. "I think God is up to something here," I said to myself. That was just the beginning. Brian was contacted by Channel 3 in Phoenix—they wanted to do a story on his Facebook post and heart-stirring response to it. By then, Brian's words had been shared almost 700 times. Now I *knew* God's hand was present!

So the KTVK cameraman and news anchor converged on our home in Wickenburg, a small town out in the desert area northwest of Phoenix that hails itself as the "Roping Capital of the World." With heavy hearts, we did our best to share what had happened and our feelings about Misty, about drugs, about loss…and about hope. Their story beautifully captured how Brian's stark words had become a vital wake-up call for addicts and their families. They interviewed a woman who had been one of Misty's friends in jail. From her prison cell, Lisa vowed that "Misty's story will inspire me to stay sober." I still remember how the story ended:

> "Misty Musick Sanchez is now saving more lives in death because of her family's courage to share the hard, hurtful truth of her addiction."

Those words gave me the chills. Misty had always wanted to help save lives. That's why she had trained to become a nurse, going back to school while working as an Emergency Room tech and raising her three sons with her husband Mark. She had even discussed going on to med school and becoming a doctor someday. One way or another, my daughter was going to help people. It's what she believed she was meant to do. Even in jail, only months before her tragic death, she had worked tirelessly to support the recovery efforts of women inmates around her. She wanted so badly to see them find the courage and confidence to get off drugs and rebuild their lives.

Unfortunately, Misty was never able to do that for herself. But could it really be true that in the aftermath of her death, my daughter could somehow play a part in saving the lives of others like her? Deep in the well of my own grief, that possibility gave me a sense of purpose and direction. Through my tears I decided to get to work! I launched my own Facebook page: "Misty Brooke Musick Sanchez: Addictions—a Painful Journey of Hope." I began posting letters that Misty and I had exchanged while she was in jail, capturing her healing, her positive spirit, and the sense of possibility about the future after she had fallen to the bottom of the pit. Going back further, I retrieved photos and notes from earlier times in Misty's life—happier, more innocent occasions before heroin addiction seized her by the throat and refused to let go. I even dusted off the pregnancy journal I kept before Misty was born on April 16, 1981.

I wanted visitors to this Facebook page to see the "real" Misty obscured under the dark cloud of addiction. I also wanted everyone to understand the loss and heartache that my husband Buddy and I, my other five children and their spouses and kids, Misty's husband and her three sons and so many others who loved Misty were suffering. I shared chronicles of my grief and how I was doing my best to go on, to lift myself out of the deep well. Like Brian, I made passionate pleas for any addicts who might happen to find me on Facebook to get help, and for families to hold on to their faith, to never give up. For family members mourning the death of a loved one to addiction, I offered my prayers and encouragement. Sometimes I presented tips or suggestions based not only on what I had learned through my experiences (positive and negative) with Misty but through my work as a professional in a treatment center for adults and adolescents suffering from eating disorders.

From the start, doors opened. Women and men whom I knew and others I had never met emerged through the network of Facebook to extend their prayers, support and appreciation for what I was trying to do. Some shared their personal memories of Misty. Those who understood what it's like to battle addiction as addicts, family members or professional helpers vowed to renew and invigorate their efforts—all in the name of Misty! As a community coming together in a common cause, we were making a statement:

This must stop! Somehow, some way, some day, addicts and those who love them will break these chains and live the lives they are meant to live.

This community, and this mission, is now extending to *you*. I am going to tell you that story of Misty and me, and I vow to be as open, honest and vulnerable as I can in sharing the love and promise, the triumphs and setbacks, the anguish and the yearning for a new start along this journey that continues on to this day.

My daughter died, but I pray that she didn't die in vain. My heart-felt wish is that she left behind seeds of hope, not through what she did do but what she did NOT do, or could not do—at least on earth. Yes, Misty really did want to save lives and perhaps telling this story may be the way to do that now. I am so sad that I don't have her voice to share with you as I had wanted to, but if I am meant to carry the baton alone, bring me to the track and point the way!

I hope that my mission will find its way into your home and your heart—whoever you are, wherever you live, and in whatever way addiction has invaded *your* life. Perhaps you are an addict still battling the demons, or an addict launching a recovery program, or family or friends of those grappling with addiction, or loved ones like our family mourning an addiction-triggered death and seeking compassion and hope for a better tomorrow. If this story makes a difference in the life of even one mother, one father, one spouse, one sibling, one child, one friend impacted by addiction, I will be proud to proclaim "mission accomplished."

I miss Misty so much, and it hurts every day. Lord knows I wish I could have saved my daughter. It's too late for that, but I hope and pray that is not too late for YOU!

CHAPTER 1

Dancing Fingers

I HAD MY daughter's name picked out long before she was even born. I don't mean a few months before her birth, but *five years* prior to bringing my baby into the world.

I was just sixteen at the time. I had a steady boyfriend, Buddy Musick, and like most teenage girls I clung to dreamy images of a happy and fulfilling future. Other girls may have been content with carving their names on a tree, but it wasn't enough for me to pick up a stone and scratch out "Buddy and Cheryl, True Love Forever" on some pine or spruce along a well-traveled path. I knew that I would marry Buddy someday, and of course I was going to have children, so my thoughts wandered much further down the road.

When the inspiration came to me, I was sitting in American History class in Richard Gahr High School in Cerritos, a southern California city not far from Long Beach. The teacher's words just sounded like blah, blah, blah to me as I doodled in my three-subject spiral notebook.

"I will marry Buddy somebody," I began. "And, oh, I'll have a little blonde-haired girl with blue eyes. And I will name her...let's see...yes, I will name her Misty Brooke Musick!"

I closed my eyes, trying to visualize this little girl, my daughter-to-come. She was wearing some cute little dress, I don't remember the color, and she was running through a field of daisies. Allowing my mind to drift further, I saw mountains in the background and a little brook alongside the field. That was the "Brooke" part of her name. I had to add the "e" at the end because I regarded myself as a creative writer and the word just needed that literary touch.

The "Misty" part of the name could be traced to a familiar scene from my early adolescence. For years I had a horse named Jethro, and often I would get a ride in the early-morning hours out to the stables where he was kept. I loved the quiet of that time of day, no one around except Jethro and me. As I approached, I would always notice the steam coming up from the barn and the dew sparkling above the grass during those beautiful moments when the sun has just begun to warm everything. Yes, my daughter would have to be "Misty."

At first, I kept my naming visualization private. But it wasn't long before I felt compelled to share it with my boyfriend. After all, he had a role to play in this scene from the future!

"I have something important to tell you," I said to Buddy. "We're going to have a daughter someday, and her name is going to be Misty Brooke Musick."

"Oh, so you've got it all picked out already?" he said, flashing a mischievous grin. He didn't offer any objections, though, which I took as full agreement. I held that name in my mind and in my heart for all the weeks, months and years ahead.

At the time, I was desperate for any kind of warm, peaceful image to carry me through my vulnerable teenage years. There had never been much warmth or peace to be found in the home that I grew up in, not with a father who kept my mother, my brothers and me in constant fear of his alcohol-induced verbal and physical abuse. As his daughter, I endured even more than that. My mother's primary response to what was happening was to drink right alongside my father. It was my first close-up encounter with addiction, and the scars would remain with me long after I left sunny California.

Buddy also had to survive a childhood with a raging alcoholic father who left his mother to raise him and his five sisters and brother when Buddy was only ten. Somehow, Buddy and I found each other, even though I was a fifteen-year-old sophomore and he was a seventeen-year-old senior attending a different high school. We met at a wedding: one of his sisters married my best friend's brother, who also happened to be Buddy's best friend.

Our first date was a Ricky Nelson concert at Knott's Berry Farm in Buena Park. In those days I was also in love with the Beach Boys, spending hours singing along to *Surfin' U.S.A.*, *Fun, Fun, Fun* and *California Girls* from the "Endless Summer" album that I proudly bought with my own money. With my long blonde hair and my attraction to the beach, I was a true California girl. Long before Buddy came along, I used to ride my bike with my friend Valerie to Seal Beach, an hour from home, or to the further shores of Huntington Beach. Before we'd dig our toes into the sand, I would visit the pharmacy around the corner and buy bars of cocoa butter to lather on my skin so I would be guaranteed to get bronzed from lounging on my beach towel in the warm California sun. I just melted into the sensations of the beach, the salt in my hair, the grainy sand under my feet and the sound of squawking seagulls as they flew above.

I loved the whole beach scene and enjoyed body surfing, but when it came to board surfing I was strictly a wannabe. I wanted to learn to surf, so one day I went with Buddy and a friend to Huntington Beach to give it a try. The two of them quickly skimmed out to deeper water while I watched for the right wave closer to shore. Paddling towards a promising swell, I turned my board around and stood up just as the wave was about to break. It was a glorious moment and my mind turned to the Beach Boys' *Surfin' USA* song just before I lost my balance and splashed into the ocean. Without a leash attached to my ankle, the board soon drifted far out of reach. Truth be told, I was not a very good swimmer, something I had not bothered to mention to Buddy. Soon after I began swimming I got tired and, although I kept telling myself "I can do this, I can do this," my brain wasn't listening to my words.

"Help! Help!" I sputtered through the foam.

Buddy and his friend were too far away to hear my cries, but to my relief and embarrassment, a good-looking, blond-haired surfer was close enough to see what was happening. After rolling his eyes, he got off his board, swam over and pulled me to safety, all the while wearing an expression that said, "Oh, brother, one of *those* again." When I got to shore I headed straight for my towel, like a puppy with my tail between my legs. While Buddy and his friend continued to surf, I decided it was safer to work on my tan.

My relationship with Buddy quickly became the primary subject of my creative writing, which I had honed under the tutelage of Miss Davis, the teacher who did radical things like allowing us to turn the classroom lights down low and write with a candle at our desks. The book that our class compiled, *In Other Words*, featured not only my writing but my accompanying art work. So I felt quite comfortable and confident putting words to my world with Buddy:

"Our love shines as the sun
And is as beautiful as the pine that we rest upon.
You turn to me and take my hand
And I can see the love glittering there on your face.
We've been together for so long,
And we've worked out the clouds of jealousy and pain.
The leaves shimmer above us
And the crystal clear water ripples nearby,
Reminding me of all the things we've shared together.
So much confusion I have gone through,
But still you come to me, you comfort me, you make me laugh.
Our love is beautiful....I watch as a piece of wood drifts slowly by
And I think of the two of us in our very own world together,
And as you touch my hand I awaken from my dream world
And you're still there sitting with me under the trees and the sky,
Your words caressing my ears, bringing me back to reality.
My chin quivers as the branches above us
And a tiny salty raindrop slides from my eyes,
As I reach for the shiny golden ring."

Our young love was no fleeting adolescent romance. Buddy and I married on July 4, 1979, which meant that we would always have fireworks celebrating our anniversary!

A year later, it was my Doberman Pinscher Cindy who seemed to know before I did that something new was brewing in my life. Cindy Bop started following me around everywhere, and when I stopped she would sit and stare at me strangely for the longest time, occasionally coming up to sniff me. She knew a secret that she couldn't tell. After I finally caught on that I was pregnant, I was hoping it would be a boy. Yes, I still had that name Misty Brooke Musick tucked away for my first-born daughter, but I thought it would be perfect to have a boy first and then a girl so he could take care of his little sister. Misty had other ideas.

Buddy and I took classes in The Bradley Method of natural childbirth. As many mothers from the late 1970s and early '80s will recall, this method preaches the right diet and plenty of exercise throughout pregnancy, with husbands trained to support their partner during labor by reminding the woman to breathe deeply. Buddy earned his "coach card" and the right to be in the delivery room when the big day arrived, and although I was assured by my doctor that it wouldn't come until May, I was already having contractions and headed for the hospital on April 16, 1981.

I kept a journal so I would always have the memory of my pregnancy and birth, not that I could ever forget one moment of it. While in labor, waiting to be moved to the delivery room, I was suffering almost unbearable pain. "Breathe, breathe," Buddy kept reminding me. I tried hard to do as I had been trained, but at some point the pain became too much and I began thrashing around on the bed. The nurse informed me in no uncertain terms that I *had* to gain control and that the baby was not getting enough oxygen. So I gathered up every ounce of strength I had left and forced myself to stay calm and continue my breathing techniques.

Then, to my relief, the contractions seemed to stop. That's when I felt the strong urge to push. It was time for my baby to come out. Well, that nurse didn't believe me at first so as the urge intensified I started to scream at her, "Let me push! Let me push!" Finally, but still too slowly for my taste, the nurse began to prepare me to be moved to the delivery room. When we passed my mother in the hallway, she held my hands as I cried.

"Mom, it hurts," I said, without time to explain the suffering I was enduring for not being allowed to push when I needed so badly to do so.

"I know," she replied.

When I was settled on the delivery table, Buddy came in all gowned and masked. At last the nurses said, "Okay, Cheryl, you can start pushing now." I think they were expecting a long, physically intense process. Ha! I pushed, and I mean I pushed hard, and after no more than three pushes the baby was on its way out.

"Look at all that hair!" Buddy exclaimed. My husband, the guy who rarely cried, had to step back, take off his glasses, and wipe his eyes. When her head popped out, they told me I could stop pushing. We heard her cry for the first time. Misty Brooke Musick had come vrooming out like a rocket as if to say, "Here I am world!"

My hands instinctively reached up to hold her, but the nurses firmly stopped me and pulled Misty away. Looking back, I suppose it was because she was messy and this was an old-school hospital operating under the belief that a baby should be cleaned off and wrapped up before being placed in its mother's arms.

When I was able to get up, I walked to the nursery to the cheers of everyone present. Buddy was strutting around like a proud rooster. We looked at our beautiful little daughter. No, she didn't have blonde hair. I forgot, there were two of us that made this baby and my husband has Italian blood, along with German and Irish, to go with the English, Dutch and French from my side. The baby that I had envisioned in my teenage daydream had in reality arrived with a head full of dark, dark hair. She looked like a little Eskimo. And the blue eyes? As I would soon discover, Misty's eyes were actually hazel. Sometimes you could see gold flecks in them.

Okay, so the physical details did not perfectly align with the picture in my mind. But my Misty was here, just as I had imagined she would be that day in history class. It was an absolute joy to take her home in her yellow and green Easter blanket, so close to my own birthday. I was blessed with the opportunity to live my dream and see what was going to come next!

A Strong-Willed Girl

Looking back, the signs of Misty's personality, aside from coming charging out of my womb on just the third push, began to show up soon after we took her home. I would put several blankets on her, believing that I had to keep her warm, but she would just throw them right off. This was a child who seemed to know just what she did and did not need.

Misty was a busy baby, which I could see at home every day. Others watched the evidence unfold every Sunday when I would insist on keeping her with me during the service at our little Baptist church. I didn't trust leaving Misty in the church nursery because after what happened to me with my father, I was determined that I would always be there to protect my daughter. So she would be with me until the crying and fussing kicked in, and then I would take her to the nursery and stay right there with her. Every Sunday, it was the same routine. Our congregation included a couple who had attended childbirth classes with Buddy and I and then had a baby boy a week after Misty's birth, in the same room I had been experiencing all that pain. Every Sunday that baby boy would sit quietly playing with his toes or peacefully sleep through the entire service. To this first-time mom, that didn't seem fair.

During our days together at home, I would rock Misty, nurse her and then lay her on the floor with her toys. She'd be fine for ten or fifteen minutes but then boom—total boredom. Oh yes, Misty could be a handful. When she started toddling at eight months, I noticed that one of her feet kind of toed in a little bit. Instead of just letting her grow out of it, her doctor put her in braces. Well, Misty was already trying to walk, having gone quickly from crawling to getting up on her feet, and those horrible braces were attached in such a way that kept her feet too spread apart. The idea was for the braces to help her feet grow properly, but all they really seemed to be doing was knock the wind out of Misty's sails. "I can't do this to her," I said as I tore them off. In reality, Misty's legs grew straight and strong and she never had an issue with them at all.

Nothing was going to slow down my little girl. In ways large and small, she made it very clear that she wanted to grow up fast. I remember often telling her in her toddler years, "Slow down, Sweetie, you're going to be an adult soon enough." When she was about four years old, I found her crouched in the bathroom trying to put a woman's pad in her underwear. "Sweetie, that's for grown women, not little girls," I calmly explained.

When Misty began making friends in preschool, she was always the boss. Wherever she led the other kids, they would be quick to follow. I found her tussling with another girl over a chair during a friend's birthday party. "Get out of my chair!" Misty barked. When she would act aggressively with other kids like that, I had to call upon every parental trick I could find to redirect her. Even when I was alone with her, there were moments when I reached my edge. When she went to touch a light socket with her finger one day, I said, "No, no, baby." When she did it again I repeated in a louder voice, "No! No!" When she did it a third time I abruptly tugged at her hand and yanked her finger back shouting, "NO! NO!" Upset by my rising anger, I was wise enough to turn to my pastor for counseling. He helped me recognize the roots of my impatience as a first-time parent.

When I was pregnant with Brian, born less than a year and a half after Misty, I found myself muttering, "Oh my gosh, how am I going to handle two of these?" As it would turn out, Brian was an easy baby in comparison and I managed to find enough energy to keep up with both him and Misty. They got along well together, enjoying their play in the sandbox that Buddy built for them, feeding the ducks at the local pond or riding the carousel at Knott's Berry Farm, the popular amusement park built out of a working farm.

Of course, all my challenges in trying to keep up with my strong-willed little girl were just part of the package in being a mother. The truth was that it was an absolute joy to have Misty in my life.

We lived in Bellflower, in Los Angeles County, in a house at the back of a long driveway with a big backyard. I remember many beautiful days when I would take Misty into that backyard where we would just sit in the shade of the trees with my Doberman Cindy and my German shepherd Chet. To keep Misty occupied, I would push her in her swing. Other days I would spend hours talking and singing to her. One song I remember was *The Long and Winding Road* by The Beatles. I took out my cassette recorder one day and recorded that song as I talked Misty through it, using the lyrics as a jump-off point to tell her over and over how much I loved her and just what she meant to me.

Misty's first birthday was a pure delight. I wrote an account of the party so she would have a memory of this milestone when she got older:

"You tried to open all of your presents and you were so funny that you made everyone laugh before Mommy ended up taking over. Daddy and Grandma took pictures, and after everyone sang 'Happy Birthday' to you, and Mommy blew out your candle, you really enjoyed digging into your cake. You were the cutest little mess." When the party continued at Farrell's ice cream shop, Misty cried when her hands got too cold from plunging into her sundae.

Before many years had passed, she would be digging her fingers into all kinds of ingredients while helping Grandma bake cookies, muffins or cupcakes. But it was another kind of activity that she would engage her hands in that would take my breath away.

A Musical Heritage

I didn't marry Buddy for his last name, but the story behind that name "Musick" and how well it fit Misty and our whole family still makes me smile. When I first met Buddy, I would kid him about his first name.

"Isn't Buddy a dog's name?" I chided. "So what's your last name?"

"Musick," he replied, carefully pronouncing it like the word "music."

"No, that can't be. Show me your driver's license," I scoffed.

Although the evidence confirmed the spelling of his name, I was still skeptical.

"No, I bet it's pronounced moo-sick, not like music, right?" I said.

When he denied this distinction, I interrogated his sister. When she backed up Buddy's story, I had to laugh. The name may not have described Buddy's family, but it was a perfect match for my own heritage.

My mother grew up in a family of musicians. My great-grandfather Peter Trottier could play a mean violin, which he called a fiddle. Self-taught, he went on to teach the violin to his daughter Mildred, my grandmother. Her sister Sarah learned to play the piano. My great-grandmother died when Mildred was only twelve, and Great Grandpa sent both girls off to live at some fancy resort where they worked during the day and performed classical music or fun ho-down tunes for guests in the evening.

Eventually, Grandma was professionally trained in classical music and mastered the piano as well as the violin. When she married Gilbert Oscar Lloyd, the musical orbit expanded. Grandpa Lloyd played anything he could get his hands on, and he mostly played by ear. As a child, I remember him picking away at his banjo as well as strumming the guitar. Both grandparents taught music and were frequently found playing gigs. Stepping into their house with my family was like entering the site of some big music festival. Assorted aunts and uncles and other relatives would show up, along with friends from the bands and orchestras my grandparents played in, or just friends who liked to jam. They'd take out guitars, banjos, pianos, violins, drums, marimbas—any instrument they could get their hands on.

My mother didn't actively follow the musical trail, but I would often find her singing some old religious hymns as she went about her chores around our house. I can still hear her singing songs like *Love Lifted Me*, *The Old Rugged Cross* and *Blessed Assurance*, with the lyrics "This is my story, this is my song, praising my Savior all the day long." I also loved to sing, and still do, so the musical strain continued to run through the veins of our family.

So it wasn't a total surprise when Buddy and I initially noticed our first-born child's natural inclination to sit down at a piano and make beautiful music. We had bought Misty one of those yellow toy keyboards, and with very little practice she began playing a very sweet *Twinkle, Twinkle*. Well, that wasn't so unusual for a young child, but then she would begin listening to songs and rush to her "piano" and play just what she had heard. The first one I remember was some Karen Carpenter song, and I watched with my mouth open as Misty practically mastered it in one take.

"What in the world? She's got the blood of Grandpa Lloyd and Great Grandpa Trottier in her!" I gushed to Buddy. Misty could not have been more than three or four years old.

So we did what any proud, supportive parents would do: we went searching for a "real" piano. Before long my grandmother found one of those old player pianos from one of her musician friends, and we got it tuned and brought it into our living room. It was a white piano, with a pad on the front to cover the opening where the bellows and the music roll once resided. The pedals were too far down for Misty to reach, but that didn't bother her. She would just swing her feet as she played. Oh, how I remember those first days of watching her little hands and tiny fingers placed so "professionally" on the keys as she crossed her ankles and swung those feet to the rhythm of the music she was creating.

Of course we also had to get her piano lessons, leading to many a recital for which Grandma would buy Misty those frilly pink and white dresses, with the patent leather shoes and socks to match. I usually preferred for Misty to dress down rather than dress up, but I had to admit the pictures of her in those frilly dresses were, and still are, pretty darn cute. Her piano teachers helped to teach her the basics while drawing out more of her natural ability, and soon she was practicing classical music on her own. I can't remember all the pieces she would play, though I would probably recognize some of them if I heard them today. One I heard recently was Beethoven's *Fur Elise*. Imagine, my little girl playing Beethoven!

Over time, Misty learned to do runs and further expand her piano-playing horizons. She could be a bit lazy with her lessons, but she never lost that zeal for hearing something she liked and immediately sitting down to play it. As she got older she would add *Amazing Grace* and other songs from church to her repertoire, and she continued to work out songs she would hear on the radio. After awhile it was like she had a large storage file of music in her head and would just sit down and play from it. Watching and listening to her make music on her piano, her fingers dancing on the keyboard, I just soaked in this part of the beauty that was Misty.

Misty just naturally played music by ear. In fact, as we would discover, she spent years fooling her piano instructors who all believed she was adept at reading music. She fooled us, too, so when a new instructor called to tell me that my daughter did not read music and would have to take some backward steps in her training to learn to do so properly, I was dubious.

"Excuse me," I said, "she's been playing all kinds of classical music and everything else she is given. She has to be reading the music."

Eventually, I was convinced. All that time when Misty was focused at the piano, paying close attention to the sheets of music in front of her, she had only been pretending to be reading the music. In truth, she was playing it all by ear, just like her great-grandfather Peter.

"Musick" was in her blood.

CHAPTER 2

—— ✂ ——

Inside the Protective Box

I DIDN'T EXPECT to have a big family. Fortunately, as nature followed her course, Buddy and I were on the same page about bringing in as much light, love and joy as we could manage, or more. After Misty and Brian, Michael came along in March 1987 and before we were finished there would be three more—Janelle, Shannon and Josh. Like most parents we were finding our way as we went along, making our fair share of mistakes. But from very early on, we held fast to one firm, unbreakable rule: no alcohol in our home!

Buddy and I didn't drink alcohol, we wouldn't serve it, and we certainly expected that as our children grew older they would have nothing to do with it either. To me, the reason was simple: alcohol was poison and evil. The horrible memories of what alcohol had done to my father, and the pain he inflicted on our family when the alcohol took hold of him, were seared into my mind, body and soul.

Even as an adult with a family of my own, I would often flash to images of my dark past. One recurring memory was that day when I was eight years old. It was a Friday, the day of the week that my father and mother would routinely come home together from Bud's Tacos after my mom finished work there and my dad had come in to drink his fill of beer at the bar. My brothers and I were used to these late Friday arrivals, and the drunken state my parents would arrive home in. On this particular Friday, however, there was no sign of our parents for hours. After it had turned dark, my fourteen-year-old brother Jeff decided to walk down the road a mile to our Uncle Mike's house to get help.

"I'm going with you!" insisted Gary, who was only seven. "No, you have to stay here," Jeff replied, but there was no stopping Gary. The two of them left, leaving me alone in the house with my brother Randy, only a few years older than me. When my parents finally stumbled through the door, my other two brothers were still gone. That didn't sit well with my father, who had consumed large amounts of whiskey this night.

"Where are they?" he yelled. "Where are your brothers?!"

My mom responded the way she usually did, trying to minimize the situation, nervously placing hamburgers on the griddle. My dad started screaming at her, but before he could do more, in walked Jeff and Gary.

"Where were you? You don't leave this house! And you took your little brother!" he shouted as he circled Jeff, his new target. Bam! My father suddenly began pounding my brother in the stomach. When my mom dared to intervene, my father immediately spun around and started hitting her with his fists. Jeff climbed on top of his father to stop him, but that only made him angrier. Like a wild boar, he threw off Jeff and charged toward my mother, pressing her backwards over the kitchen counter with his strong hands around her neck.

I had seen my father's rage many times before, but never like this. I watched breathlessly as he began choking my mother, and when my eye caught the knives on the counter and her hand inching toward them, I screamed.

Now I became the target! With fire in his eyes, my father stormed toward me. My mother managed to stagger over to head off the beast, and as punishment for interfering; he smashed her head through the window, shattering the glass. Somehow she emerged without blood pouring from her body and scrambled to rescue me from his fury. After he chased me through the kitchen, I managed to bolt outside, propelled by one thought: *Call the police! I've got to get to our neighbor and call the police!* I never made it that far. When he caught up to me, he ordered me back inside and kicked me down the hallway. Though I'm sure the noise carried far outside our walls, no one bothered to call the police. And the terrifying night continued....

I wish I could say that was the only haunting memory that would come crackling through my brain over the years, but that wasn't the case at all. Beyond the violence I also endured a long pattern of sexually inappropriate language and behavior. I specifically recall one time, at age five, that my father did touch me while 'tucking me into bed'. Other times he tried to kiss me on the lips, peep through the keyhole, or walk into the bathroom when I was in the tub. If anyone dared to question his actions, he would laugh, shake his head and proclaim, "Sorry, It was just an accident." But I knew he did it purposely. One drunken night I heard my father make a vow that he "would see her naked before she got married" and nothing or no one was going to stop him. Nor could I see any way to prevent him from routinely entering my bedroom late at night, when he would just hover over my bed in the dark. Sometimes I noticed him tiptoeing inside, and sometimes I would wake up to find him lurking there. I didn't have to suffer the actual physical act to feel as if I had been raped. Hour after hour, I would force myself to stay awake, knowing that if I let down my guard he would make me pay.

I knew that much of what my father did was because of alcohol. For a short time I partied with my friends, and one particular night I drank hard liquor from a bar at the home of my friend Vicki. Gulping down shots of vodka and tequila the way I had watched my father guzzle his booze, I wound up passed out the entire evening. I had consumed so much alcohol in such a short amount of time, it's a wonder I didn't die. After that frightening experience, I was wise enough to never try that again; however I did take a liking to champagne and found that, rather than a glass; I would drink the entire bottle, and then go for another. I began to realize I may have the same addictive tendencies as my parents.

So when I found myself with my own children, there was never a question about whether they would ever see me take a drink. Buddy felt just as committed about this. We both vowed that what we had been forced to witness and experience in our alcohol-shrouded households would never happen in our house. *Never.*

Yes, we would shield our children from the abuses of alcohol. But I decided that I would take my protection a step further: Misty and her brothers and sisters would be safe from any and all kinds of inappropriate conduct at the hands of any adult figure in their lives. Somehow or other, I would wrap them inside a protective box where nothing or no one could harm them. Like many mothers, I saw myself as a lioness out to protect her cubs, and I took that role *very* seriously. No matter where we lived, or how much money we had, or what challenges we would face, I would always be that lioness....

In those early years of raising our kids, I still maintained a relationship with my father. He was my children's grandfather, after all, and although I would be hyper-vigilant about letting Misty or the others wander off alone with him, I believed he had a right to be a part of their lives. He and my mother lived a couple of houses down from us in Bellflower, so naturally they were invited when I planned a big celebration for the Fourth of July in 1987.

Buddy and I didn't call that day our wedding anniversary, even though it was, because to everyone else July 4th was just a fun holiday. For this Fourth, I was going all out. My younger brother Gary, who survived that house of horrors growing up as we all somehow had done, was there, along with dozens of friends and neighbors from the nearby duplexes and triplexes. Priding myself as a creative activities coordinator, I decked out our property with American flags and balloons, and we dressed up the kids in red, white and blue clothes for our own Fourth of July parade.

Since Misty was six and Brian was four, they fit right in the celebration while I had my hands full with four-month-old Michael. The grown-up guys showed off their barbecue skills with the hamburgers, chicken and hot dogs, and with the potato salad and the corn on the cob and the cakes and pies, everyone had their fill. Soon after the plates were scraped clean, many of the adults and some of the kids were playing volleyball around the net that I had put up for the celebration. Some of the men chose to play a little pickup basketball at the hoop that my dad had just bought and mounted. He was proud of that hoop and was giving his all in the game. I was inside with my mom when one of the neighbors rushed in from out back.

"Where's the phone? Where's the phone?" he panted.

"What, what's going on?" I asked. Turning toward my mother he muttered, "It's your husband."

Bolting outside, I found Buddy at my father's side, taking his pulse. Dad was just lying there staring up at Buddy and when I crouched down he turned his gaze toward me. His half-open eyes were dilating. "Dad! Dad!" I shouted. Then I watched his eyes close. The next few minutes became a blur of Buddy and Gary and maybe others frantically trying to perform CPR and then the ambulance coming and my dad being taken away. Unbeknownst to all of us then, his alcoholism, smoking, large consumption of greasy food and general unhealthy lifestyle had contributed to arteriosclerosis. The heart attack was fatal.

"Is Grandpa going to heaven?" Misty asked when the commotion settled down.

"Yes, Misty, Grandpa is going to heaven now" her grandmother responded, because that was enough of an answer for a six-year-old girl. But, in my heart I wondered. When I got back from the hospital, Brian greeted me with a different question: "Mommy is it time to do the fireworks now?" As he looked at me expectantly with his big brown eyes, I was able to take a breather from the shock and sadness. *How nice to be four years old,* I thought as I took my son's hand.

Despite all the suffering my father had brought to my home growing up, I still loved him. I mourned his death on that day, my eighth wedding anniversary, but I was soon caught in the family strain churned up after his heart attack. There had always been major stress in our family wherever my father and his alcoholism was involved, and now it shifted to funeral arrangements, questions about Mom's living situation and other practical matters. I just wasn't feeling good about where any of it was headed. That's when the idea began to form for a major change regarding how we would raise our family...and where.

"I think we need to get out of here," I said to Buddy one night.

As I was feeling a push out the door of California, I also began feeling a pull toward somewhere new. Our friends Robert and Sue Goldenberg extended an invitation for us that we had to seriously consider. They had been friends at our California church, where "Pastor Bob" had been serving as associate pastor, and he had recently accepted the opportunity to become pastor of the Christian and Missionary Alliance Church in Wickenburg, Arizona.

"Come to Wickenburg and join our community," he urged. "It's beautiful here. You'll love it. And we're looking for youth leaders. You and Buddy could step right in."

I had never even heard of this little Arizona town, but I figured we could at least make a visit and check it out. It was good to get away, even for a little while, and the Goldenberg's were gracious hosts. Late one evening Buddy and I found ourselves outside looking up at the stars in the perfectly clear skies. In smog-shrouded southern California, you never got a clear view of the stars.

"Are you feeling what I'm feeling?" I said as I turned toward my husband. "We are really supposed to come out here to live, aren't we? God's calling us here."

Buddy nodded. This was a spiritual tug, something I was much more receptive to since I had returned to church after a brief void of religious practice while struggling with my painful childhood. I knew that moving would bring many challenges, especially considering that Buddy would have to give up the mobile vehicle repair business that had been sustaining us after he had been laid off from a well-paying job. He had no employment prospects awaiting him in Wickenburg. We were acting on faith—God had a better plan for Buddy and me, and especially for Misty, Brian, Michael and the kids that would follow them. This move seemed perfectly aligned with my priorities. The safe protective box that I so badly wanted to wrap my family in would hold up much better away from busy, overcrowded and sometimes dangerous Los Angeles County.

So there we were, a few days after Christmas and less than six months after my father's heart attack, loading up a moving van, Buddy's truck, and our car and heading east toward the Arizona border. Well, if God were calling us, I guess He decided He would test our commitment along the way. Randy was driving Buddy's work truck, filled with the tools Buddy used in his automotive repair business. About halfway along the trip, the truck broke down. After Randy and Buddy huddled, they mapped out a plan: Randy would stay with the truck while Buddy drove the van all the way to Wickenburg, where he would quickly drop off some of our belongings, along with me and the three kids, before backtracking to where he had left Randy. Then they would get the truck fixed up or towed and get back on the road, and one way or another they would complete our big family move.

That was the plan anyway. Buddy wanted to make good time, of course, but when the baby started to get hungry and I started to get a case of white line fever while driving the car with Misty and her two siblings in it, he agreed to stop for dinner. So I got the baby fed and the rest of us managed to eat something before our scaled down caravan resumed and finally rolled into Wickenburg. Buddy stayed just long enough to unload some of the furniture from the moving van before turning right around and heading back to find Randy.

At least we had been dropped at the home we would be renting. Unfortunately, in the rush-rush state Buddy and I parted in, we were left with no clean clothes and little or nothing in the way of handy food options. Brian had wet himself while sleeping and the rest of us were exhausted and disoriented. As someone who had grown accustomed to having my mother on call from practically next door in California, I was not exactly a pillar of stone in those first hours in our new town, especially when I knew that my husband was driving alone for several hours west on the highway—with no sleep. I needed help, and fast. With Michael in my arms and Misty and Brian in tow, I knocked on our neighbor's door. A kind-looking woman answered.

"Hello, you don't know me but we're moving here from California and my little boy is wet and we have no clothes for him and I just don't know what to do right now," I stammered. It couldn't have been much later than dawn.

"Well, you come right on inside," she said. "You folks just rest. I'll fix you something."

She pulled out some clothes belonging to her grandson that fit Brian perfectly. One need met. Then she fixed us all pancakes.

"Oh my gosh, thank you," I managed to say between gulps while monitoring the kids' syrup pouring. "After all we went through last night; you don't know how good this feels."

It wasn't long before I was spilling out the rest of my worries. I had not heard from Buddy all night or that morning. Where was he? Had something happened? Our new neighbor explained that she knew a couple of Wickenburg police officers, and soon they began making calls to highway patrol and hospitals along Buddy's route... just to make sure.

As I would finally learn, Buddy had never even made it to Randy the night before. He had pulled into a rest stop, devoured a quick snack, gulped down some Pepsi, and fell fast asleep—with the moving van's engine still running and the heater on. Mid morning, he woke up, got to Randy, and worked everything out. The kids and I, bolstered by the hospitality of our neighbor, were nourished and rested. When the trucks and our men finally reached us, an armada of neighbors and folks from the Goldenberg's church were showing up at our door with food, clothing and an endless stream of smiles and hugs.

It was New Year's Day 1988. I thanked God for the New Year, our new home and the new beginnings that awaited us. Already we were warmed by the kind of hospitality that we had seldom experienced in California. It was as if everyone had pooled together and created a symbolic sign that said "Welcome to Wickenburg."

We would never look back.

I can't say that I fully appreciated all the ways of small-town living right away in Wickenburg, which had about 7,000 residents year-round with a swelling of double that size during the snowbird months from October to May. Early one evening I was taking a walk alone while Buddy watched Misty and her siblings. I was casually strolling along a country road into what I just called "the desert" because, as I was quickly finding out, almost any land outside the main streets of town could be considered desert. The first few people who rode by me, or whom I passed by, all turned to me and waved.

Well, I didn't know any of these people, and back home in Los Angeles County you don't wave at strangers. As my heart began to beat more rapidly, I said to myself, "Where is there a safe house I can rush inside?" Then I paused. "Wait, this isn't California," I said to myself. "People just wave at you here!" Waving was their way of telling me I was welcome to walk where I was walking, that they considered me a friend even though they didn't know me, and that rather than being a threat to harm me they would be watching my back. My new home was going to be much safer and friendlier than Bellflower. How refreshing was that?

Then I would turn on the news. In California, we had gotten used to watching and reading the daily bombardment of violent crime, with images of screeching sirens and foreboding helicopters hovering overhead. Sometimes we wouldn't even have to turn on the news to find reminders of violence and mayhem because they were all around us, as much a part of everyday life in southern California as the smog and the earthquakes. In Wickenburg, I would pick up the newspaper and read the latest "crime" report pulled from the police blotter: "Mrs. Olson's flower pot got cracked in front of her business. It looks like some child might have dumped it over."

Sometimes the contrast between Wickenburg and Los Angeles County was so striking I had to laugh, even if that meant risking being called a "haughty Californian." My new friends and neighbors wanted to show off Coffinger Park, the town's main recreational area. In California we were spoiled by lush, green, carefully mani-cured public parks. At my first sight of our new town's park, I blurt-ed out, "Are you kidding me?" What I saw was lots and lots of dirt, with a few patches of grass here and there, a rough looking base-ball diamond, a tiny swimming pool and a playground with rusty, outdated equipment.

I also had to learn important lessons about the climate of the Arizona desert during summer. During our first months there I took a temporary part-time job at the Wickenburg Inn, which at the time was one of the town's primary dude ranches and would later be owned by Merv Griffin. Wickenburg was once known as the "Dude Ranch Capital of the World" and the guest ranch industry was still one of the main sources of local employment then. Part of my job was to come in early in the morning to feed and water the horses in the stables, preparing them for rides later in the day. Then I would saddle the horses; assist the guests who were scheduled to ride by assigning them a horse and getting them mounted. I would take the guests out on a beautiful trail ride, return, water the horses and take out another group of riders. As I soon discovered, even in the hours just before and after sunrise it would get pretty darn hot on the av-erage summer day in Wickenburg, where it was not unusual for the temperature to soar well over 110 degrees. On one of my first morn-ings on the job, I began feeling dizzy. Although not yet aware that dizziness was one of the first signs of heat exhaustion, I was smart enough to stand aside for a moment and drink some water. To my surprise, someone was watching me and waiting to set me straight.

"A good wrangler takes care of the horses first, not themselves," my supervisor informed me. So I promptly headed back out in sun-shine to water the herd and finish the job. By the time I arrived home I was pale and sick. Not wanting to lose this first job while Buddy was scrambling to make money, I figured I needed to adopt better tactics to deal with the heat. That's when I learned to wet my hair and put ice cubes under my wide brimmed western hat to keep cool while staying on task with the horses.

I learned that Wickenburg rose up as a community in 1863 when German prospector Henry Wickenburg came around during the gold strike and discovered the Vulture Mine, where $30 million in gold was dug from the ground over the years. Mr. Wickenburg was Mister Everything, serving the new town as judge, Justice of the Peace, school inspector and president of the mining district. Apparently he got swindled out of most of his fortune, and when he died by gunshot in 1905 there were conflicting stories as to whether he shot himself or someone else pulled the trigger, stories that became part of our Western lore. The Wickenburg that our family entered was a friendly, easy-going community where people looked out for each other.

To Buddy and I, this was the perfect place to raise Misty and the rest of our family. It would blend smoothly with my plan to keep our close-knit family safe and secure, protected from the dangers of the world. Of course, we understood that the town would not function as an effective protective shield alone. The environment that we created under our own roof would always be our first line of defense. I had my protective box to assemble and maintain, and I was all-in for the mission. As Misty and her siblings would discover, banning alcohol from the premises was just the starting point.

For many years in Wickenburg we struggled financially. Buddy scrambled to find work, starting with a job as a janitor, and after my very brief stint at the guest ranch I resumed my commitment to stay home with the kids until Misty was safely escorted into late adolescence. We never had money for any kind of extras. When the girls at our church were expected to wear fancy dresses, I explained that "If I have to choose between a gallon of milk for my family or a fancy dress, I'm going to get the milk." Our money shortfalls were so frequent that an aunt asked me, "Are you sure God told you to move to Wickenburg?" Yes, I was sure.

In fact, I thought it was important that we always express gratitude for what we *did* have. We got evicted from the home we were first renting after we couldn't keep up with the rent and, because it happened in October when the snowbirds were flocking to town, available housing options in our price range were almost impossible to turn up. The only thing we could find was a dingy place no bigger than a bachelor's apartment, with no cupboard space and no room for our dogs—they would have to be chained outside. As we prepared to cram inside, the kids were asking what on earth we were going to do in such a tiny space.

"I'll tell you what we're going to do," I said. "First, we are going to praise God for having a roof over our heads so we don't have to live on the street. Then we are going to get out the buckets and start cleaning our new home." Then I began to pray. "Dear Lord, thank you for providing walls to protect us from the weather and a ceiling above us to keep out the rain." Just as I grabbed the buckets and cleaning supplies, the phone rang.

"I heard you're looking for a good place to rent," the caller said. It was someone Buddy had met, the husband of a sweet older couple. "Well, I've got a place out here behind the Safeway. I'm going to be selling it but I figured I would rent it in the meantime. Would you like to come out and take a look?"

Did we? It was a perfect house for us, with plenty of room outside in the dirt and stones for the kids to play in, as well as hills to ride their bikes, trees to climb and spaces to make forts. The dogs had plenty of room to roam. It was small, with not nearly enough bedrooms for a growing family, but I figured that's why bunk beds were invented. For years that house didn't sell; it truly became our home. We even kept a small chicken coop and had our own fresh eggs.

I was always on the lookout for ways to have fun and for rituals to keep us close. Buddy put up a swing set along with a sandbox. When the rains washed the grounds, we'd go out to form perfect mud puddles. The kids would hunker down in the mud and I would get right down in there with them, with pans selected from the kitchen for the important task at hand: making mud pies! After that activity, it would be time to clean up and head back indoors to bake cookies, with dough and chocolate chips to plunge our hands into instead of mud.

In the evening I liked to bring the kids together to read by the fireplace in the large great room. Over time, I read through the entire series of *Little House on the Prairie*, more than once. As Christmas approached, before we discovered Buddy's allergic reaction to pine, we would bundle up the kids to go out in search of the perfect tree. As soon as we brought it home, I would start the milk on the stove to make hot chocolate, which our family liked to stir with candy canes for that mint taste. I would also serve another family favorite: popcorn with Doritos. Misty especially loved that tradition, savoring the taste of the Doritos warmed by the popcorn. To decorate the tree, each family member would put on their own special ornament first and then it would be free time to keep decorating.

When Christmas Eve arrived, I would take out my well-worn copy of *The Animals' Christmas Eve* and read it to the children huddled by the Christmas tree, after a dinner of finger food and a very important ritual: lighting candles and singing "Happy Birthday" to Jesus before each child blew out one candle each. Everyone could pick out one present to open on Christmas Eve, with the rest saved for Christmas morning when we would enjoy coffee cake while everyone took turns opening presents, with the stockings saved for last.

Since we couldn't afford adventurous vacations, I always kept my eye out for ways to create meaningful memories at home. When Misty's twelfth birthday came, I came up with a real winner! The event is still known today as "Misty's Pig Pen Party." I have to admit that I borrowed this idea from a magazine before adding personal touches to it. For a family with a tradition of rolling around in the mud and making mud pies, a pig pen party just seemed to fit. The concept was to come to the party wearing clothes that you didn't mind getting dirty, and then go home from the party in the filthiest state you could get yourself in.

I bought some pink felt and hand-sewed two pig noses out of them, using elastic to hold them on. They would serve as prizes for the pig pen king and queen. I used a headband to attach pig ears, and I bought a big, plastic piggy bank, along with a fluffy toy stuffed pig. So the kids had a great incentive to dive in and get filthy!

The carefully selected menu included forkless spaghetti and fork-less cake, and my mother stood by with a ladle doling out the cup-less punch. "I'm just an oooold lady, I don't know all those fancy ways to serve punch," she would say as she wobbled that ladle and poured the liquid over their faces. To complement the forkless cake I added spoon-less chocolate pudding to the dessert offerings.

Misty had invited all her friends, and her siblings also had the opportunity to get down and dirty too. Activities included a mud roll, a food fight and the ultra-popular reverse food fight. For that event, the kids got to squirt themselves from a plentiful supply of mustard, ketchup, pudding and the rest of the spaghetti. As a mother, I can say that there is nothing quite like the sight of children grabbing huge gobs of spaghetti and plopping it on their heads—and not have to reprimand them for their horrible manners!

We chose a king and a queen of the pig pen, who happily posed for a photo-op while touching their pig noses in an Eskimo kiss. The party attendee judged to be "The Filthiest Pig," got to take home that big pink plastic piggy bank. For many years afterward, no matter where life may have taken them, when Misty's girlfriends got together they would be quick to say, "Remember that party your mom gave you? Oh my God, that was so much fun!"

We created many more fun memories as our family grew, with Misty's sisters Janelle and Shannon born in the early '90s. By then we were a family of five kids pushing the space limits of the home that we loved. The bedroom Buddy and I slept in was barely big enough for our bed and dresser, and the kids were squeezed in their bunks in one open room. Janelle was in a crib and Shannon in a bassinet, and there was simply no place left to put anyone.

Once again, God provided. By then Buddy was operating a small gym and fitness center, where I would help out on a limited part-time basis. Money was still scarce, but our vulnerable financial state actually opened a door to us. In 1995 we were selected to become the first family in Wickenburg to have a Habitat for Humanity home built just for us! It turned out to be perfect timing because I was pregnant again, with Josh arriving late that summer. By next spring, our new house—our very own home—was ready for the Musick family to move into. On April 20, 1996 the media referred to us as "The First Family of Wickenburg" and I wrote a poem for the big day titled "Standing at the Door Looking In":

Standing at the door looking in
I can almost smell the warm fragrance
Of cookies baking in the oven.
I can almost feel a little hand tugging at my shirt,
Eager for that first crumbly bite.
Standing at the door looking in
I can almost hear the voices of children
Giggling in their room down the hall.
I can almost hear the laughter, the crunching snacks
As a card game is played around the table.
Standing at the door looking in
I can almost feel wet tears on my shoulder
As I bandage a scraped knee.
I can almost hear the gentle creak creaking
And smell the sweetness of baby being rocked to sleep.
Standing at the door looking in
I can almost smell the aroma of pine
As I watch the children decorate the tree.
I can almost hear the corn popping,

See the blinking of Christmas lights,
And hear excited voices chatter.
Standing at the door looking in
I can almost feel the joy and pride
Of a graduation and a wedding.
I can almost feel the breathless excitement
As each family member rushes to be ready on time.
Someday, memories of a little hand tugging at my shirt
Will flood my heart and mind
As I stand at the door looking in.

Sharing a home that we loved, no matter the size or shape, was an essential part of building that safe, protective box I had to create for Misty and our whole family. The rituals and fun parties had their place too. Another component of the glue that kept us together and on the right path was our Christian faith and the churches where we celebrated.

It was a church and our connections with the people in it that had first paved our path to Wickenburg. Initially, we joined the church led by Pastor Bob, our friend from California. He and his wife Sue had young kids close to Misty and Brian's age, so our families naturally bonded. Buddy and I both helped out with the church's youth program for awhile. However, conflicts began to sprout up, as they can do even in a church with people you care about and who care about you. Though we left on unhappy terms, we remained friends with the Goldenberg's even after they moved out of Wickenburg for a new ministry in the East.

For awhile we were between churches and even hosted worship services in our home after Buddy was ordained through the Home Ministry Fellowship. Before long, though, we were drawn to join a new community with Pastor Duane Middleton at Mount Hope Assembly of God. He was just launching his ministry at the time, so when our family began attending the services he would joke that "the Musicks have just doubled our congregation." It wasn't long before the young woman who was handling the children's ministry left and Pastor Duane turned to me and asked, "Could you take this over for us now?" Soon I was named Director of the Children's Church and began to come up with creative ways to nurture kids from kindergarten up through middle school years. I began filling the nursery with my own artwork, progressing from drawing animals to capturing people's faces. I helped advance a popular church project of having all the kids leave their handprints in paint on the walls of the corridor outside the nursery. The kids called me "Mrs. Cheryl" and I even won the Sunday School Teacher of the year several times. When Misty was a preteen, she helped me out with the younger kids before the church got a youth program up and running.

As Mount Hope grew, the energy at the Sunday services began rising. Music was a focal point, with the congregation singing in full voices and lifting their hands in praise or resonance with the pastor's message. I embraced the Pentecostal foundation and passionate tone, and I made sure that all my kids attended. Over the years Mount Hope would play a central role in the ongoing story of Misty and our whole family—in both good ways and bad.

This is where my story of maintaining the protective box that would hold Misty and my other children in a safe cocoon gets…difficult to bring up. You see, I believed with all my heart at that time that for any of us, loving Jesus and devoting our lives to Him sets the right direction for our life path. I *still* believe that. Yet, as I look back at some of my choices and attitudes as a mother, I now recognize that there were ways in which I was over the top with the way I practiced Christianity. I clung to a single-minded focus to make that safe, protective bubble take the form of a perfect Christian box, leading to unintended but harmful consequences.

Determined to keep my kids away from all evil, I would often act out of fear. When Misty invited her friend Liz over to our house for sleepovers, I was quick to say yes. I liked Liz and could see that Misty enjoyed her company. But when Liz and her mother asked permission for Misty to come to stay over at *their* house, my reply was a firm "no." I just didn't know Liz's father well; I wasn't sure he was living a devout Christian life. Maybe I was afraid that he could turn out to be someone who approached young girls the way my father behaved with me, and I simply could not take that chance. It didn't matter to me that Misty didn't like my decision and Liz's mom felt offended. I wasn't budging. I just kept repeating to myself, "If I can just keep her close to me, nothing bad will happen to her."

Misty was my first-born and she would always be safe. I was quick to embrace any and all evidence of her innocence and purity, like the essay she wrote for school as a twelve-year-old called "Three Wishes":

> If I had the power to make three of my wishes come true it would probably take me a long time to decide which ones I should wish for. My first wish would be for wisdom. So much wisdom that I could help solve our nation's problems, wisdom that would get me somewhere in the world. My next wish would be generosity to everyone. Maybe if people had generosity there wouldn't be homeless or neglected people. If rich people were generous there wouldn't be as many poor people. My final wish would be openness to God and his word. It hurts me to see people swimming in their sins. So hurt by other people that they aren't themselves anymore. With openness to God I would see more people strive for an eternity with Christ instead of just not caring.

I was determined that this innocence, this spirit of kindness and generosity, and this devotion to her faith would never be taken away from Misty. When she reached middle school age, I decided to homeschool her to shield her from the evil influences lurking in the public school environment. I was going to keep her "clean," which was, after all, part of the reason that I had chosen to be a stay-at-home mom. I was always going to be there to supply that added layer of protection. Well, it only took a brief experiment to realize that Misty simply didn't have the temperament to thrive under the home-school approach, and neither did I. I had to bring her back to school.

When I discovered that Misty had started sneaking cigarettes when she was only about fourteen, I panicked. Smoking certainly did not fit inside my perfect Christian family box! For awhile I would stalk her. Would I catch her in the act of smoking again? Would I smell the evidence on her breath? If I did, there would be swift consequences. I was also vigilant about her friends, hoping they all would emerge from our church community. So it was reassuring when she began spending time with Pastor Duane's daughter Carissa, a year older than Misty.

Of course, I recognized that boys might soon enter into the picture. I was determined to come up with an idea for something that would help give my daughter the strength to enter this world with the right attitude and beliefs. The light bulb went off: a chastity ring! Her daddy would give Misty this symbolic ring and she would remain chaste until she was married. That would be one more important way to keep Misty in that safe, protective box.

So one day the three of us dressed up in the nicest clothes we could afford and we took Misty out to dinner. It was a special way for us to show her how much we loved her and were firmly committed to stand by her as she began to walk the path of truly becoming a young lady. As Buddy slipped the chastity ring on Misty's finger, he proclaimed, "The next man to take this off will be your husband." It was a beautiful moment, assuring me that one of my dreams for my precious daughter would be fulfilled.

When Misty began to show interest in Andy, she was still only fourteen. My antennae went up, but I could at least comfort myself in knowing that this was boy was active in the ministries at Mount Hope too. Of course, we didn't like that he was seventeen because three years is a pretty significant age difference with adolescent boys and girls. Still, he seemed like a nice boy and we did allow him to visit Misty at our home.

"Okay, you guys can hold hands, period," Buddy and I announced. Of course, when we would leave the house for a brief grocery run we would find out much later that they had been making out hot and heavy while we were gone. "I don't want to listen to your rules," Misty seemed to be saying, which threw me into a worrying spiral. I had to keep that protective box intact and sturdy. One morning while lying in bed, I had a strong sense come over me, prompting me to bolt up. "Misty is no longer a virgin!" a voice informed me. I ran out of our bedroom to the bathroom where Misty was leaning over the sink putting on her mascara.

"Misty," I said firmly, "the Lord told me that you are no longer a virgin. Sweetie, is that true?" She dropped the wand into the sink without speaking the words that I already knew. I didn't yell at her or slam the door and walk away in disgust. Instead, I just came up to her and held her close.

"I still love you. You're still our precious child," I said, but later that morning I drove around Wickenburg alone, weeping, "I just lost my baby!" I had not experienced grief like that since suffering a miscarriage between two of my six children.

After Misty shared what had happened with Andy during a private talk with her grandma, Buddy and I decided that we needed to confide in Pastor Duane. This was a spiritual matter of high importance! Pastor Duane arranged a meeting to be led by Mount Hope's youth minister, Duane's brother Melvin. He knew both Misty and the boy. Buddy and I were brought in to meet with this "boyfriend."

"Do you know why you're here?" Melvin asked the young man.

"Why?" he asked, feigning innocence.

"Andy, tell the Musicks what you need to tell them," Melvin said sternly.

After a long pause, Andy cleared his throat.

"Misty and I had sex," he said finally.

As the details gradually spilled out, I learned that it wasn't even a warm, affectionate first-time sexual experience for my little girl. Misty and Andy had physically joined together in an outhouse on a construction site near our home. Misty would claim, although not strongly, that he forced himself on her. Based on the behavior we had witnessed with the two of them earlier, I wasn't so sure about that. Mostly I just felt a deep, deep sadness.

Our intervention didn't end with that meeting at church. We had asked Misty to give back her chastity ring because now, as if she were somehow dirty or soiled. "That's my ring! This is not right!" Misty argued, but she relented. She had no choice.

The next scene of our family drama was played out in public one Sunday at Mount Hope. During the altar service, with the music pounding and people shouting "Praise you, Jesus!" Misty was visibly crying. "*She's repenting*!" I thought to myself, and a sense of joy and optimism spread over me. Maybe my dream for my daughter could be salvaged. So we made a scene of crying with her and praying over her. With people all around us tuning in to what we were doing, I held Misty's hands high in the air in triumph and celebration. And at that moment Buddy slipped the chastity ring back on Misty's finger. Praise you, Jesus!

In my mind, we had made a clear and powerful statement: we were, in a spiritual sense giving our daughter's purity back to her. As she continued to cry, I still believed she was simply moved by what was happening, that she was truly returning to Jesus and the plan He had for her life. As we were leaving church, a man she knew in the congregation pointed his finger at her and said, "Misty, get it together or you're going to hell!" I nodded in approval. As we walked toward the car, I added, "Look how much he loves and cares about you, Misty!"

That is how that Sunday morning scene unfolded, but as I write those words and remember the experience that day I wish with all my heart that I could turn back the hands of time and rip that scene out of my memory vault. The reality is that I just didn't get it that Sunday at Mount Hope Assembly of God church. I didn't get it for a long time afterward. It took me many years, and many painful parenting lessons, to discover the truth of what was actually happening that day. What my daughter Misty had been subjected to then was nothing less than religious abuse, plain and simple. She was humiliated. And her mother had not only stood by and allowed it all to happen but had been a willing and active participant. Caught in some kind of Cinderella syndrome and my rigid Christian mindset, I just didn't recognize that while Misty was crying out for compassion and understanding she was instead receiving shaming and blaming.

I can't erase that past experience with Misty, just as I can't wipe away other choices that I would later question or regret. I can at least comfort myself in remembering that that there would be many brighter days for Misty and me, and for our family, after that misguided moment. We still created fun memories; we still observed our favorite family traditions. Misty went on to enjoy many positive experiences at church, including an opportunity to join a youth group's mission to Mexico where she was able to participate in delivering food, clothing and bicycles to low income families. When she came home, she told me that she had learned that "the more poor people are, the more willing they are to share whatever they have, even if it's just a little bit of beans and rice." The spirit of her "Three Wishes" essay was still present inside my daughter.

Still, as Misty advanced through the vulnerable teenage years, we would witness more and more signs that this was a girl determined to live life on her own terms. She was a free spirit, a reality that was not easy for me to accept. My belief at that time was that as a mother in a Christian family, if you teach them the Bible, take them to church and do your best to show them the right example, they will just naturally turn out okay. And if Misty and all my kids turned out right, my goal would be fulfilled: to create a structured, peaceful, and healthy home after being raised in a household of chaos and dysfunction.

As the years went by, however, I would be forced to consider a different and frightening reality: maybe there is no such thing as a perfect home or a perfect Christian family. If I closed my eyes and visualized the physical presence of that protective box I hoped to keep Misty safely inside of, I could almost see her feet pushing up against the lid, with Mommy holding her hand firmly on top in a vain attempt to keep her down in there. The more Misty would push to get out, the harder I would fight to keep her inside.

It would be a long time before I could accept the truth that where Misty was concerned, I was never going to be able to keep the lid on that protective box. It would be even longer until I realized that it probably wasn't my place to even try. Sometimes as a mother you just have to understand that you can't keep them from evil; you can't control them. You simply have to let go...and let God be God.

CHAPTER 3

———— ✿ ————

Her Own Kind of Music

"MISTY HAS A voice that melts like butter."

Those were the words of the youth pastor at Mount Hope Assembly of God church while Misty was participating in a teen trio with Pastor Duane's daughter Carissa and their friend Lisa. It was nice to hear the compliment, but Misty's rich alto voice had already been melting my heart every time I would listen to her sing at our piano or watch her in the many singing competitions she excelled in. When she hit the high notes while our family was doing our best to harmonize on *Silent Night* on Christmas Eve, it felt like her voice was shooting right up to heaven.

Singing was simply another of Misty's many musical gifts. She still played the piano and had learned the clarinet, but it was that voice that had begun to attract the attention of everyone who heard her. Pastor Duane recognized her potential right away. He was a natural musician himself as singer, pianist and bass player so he was thrilled to have the opportunity to launch a choir with Misty a key part of it. His own voice ranged high enough for him to sing soprano and alto so he could help teach the girls.

"I don't give you the music. I want you to *feel* it," he told Misty. "Just open your mouth and let it out!"

Misty thrived with that kind of freedom, and with a perfect blend of a theatrical presence and a Pentecostal energy, Mount Hope's choir soared to surprising heights. Not only did they consistently elevate our church's observance of important religious events such as Palm Sunday and Resurrection Sunday, they also took their talents beyond our walls. Misty and her friends achieved the Superior level at a state

Fine Arts competition, which qualified them for a national competition in St. Louis. Misty loved every minute of it.

At school, her singing ability carried her to first chair at Regional's and second chair in the Arizona State Choir. She was winning new awards for her singing all the time. Just as important to her proud mother, Misty's musical accomplishments and enthusiasm was helping to inspire her siblings to actualize the musical influences in their heritage. It often seemed that the Musicks really were all about music.

Brian was a natural with the guitar, though his affinity for heavy metal and his hair extending down toward his waist would challenge his parents' concerns. As Michael grew older he would opt for a blue Mohawk, which he glued into tall, edgy liberty spikes at times—hairstyle was one area where we actually allowed our kids to make choices way outside my protective box—as he mastered his trumpet and talked of joining a Ska band that performed reggae-like music. Janelle loved the cello and also learned to play the small violin that she inherited from my grandmother, who had learned to play it when she was only seven. "Take good care of this violin. When I was young it was my best friend," Janelle's great-grandma told her. Shannon took the acoustic guitar that I couldn't master and began earning tips at open mic nights and even doing backup for hip-hop acts. Josh, our youngest, would turn heads in church when he kept up a perfect beat while "drumming" on back of the pews, or his pant leg to any music being played on stage, providing an early preview of his drumming performances as a teenager. Many of these musical endeavors wouldn't flourish until Misty had left home, but as the first-born she blazed the trail in our family for the musical expression that ran through the veins of my ancestors.

For awhile, that trail appeared to have no limits for my daughter. "I can see a bright future for Misty in music," Pastor Duane would say. "She could become a musical director some day, or maybe a performance artist. She can do so much with her God-given ability."

That's what I believed, too, and oh how I wanted that kind of bright future for my daughter, whether it happened to be in music or some other profession. At home Misty still loved to play the piano that my mother had purchased in the wake of my father's heart attack and then passed on to our family to support Misty's potential and our family's love of sharing music at home. Although Misty lost some steam in her formal piano lessons after her local Wickenburg teacher admitted that "I've gone as far as I can with her," she still sat down at the keyboard for the immense pleasure it brought to her and to those who heard her play. There was simply no denying Misty's ability to entertain and delight people through music. Add to that her intelligence, her engaging personality and her generous spirit and you could just sense the wonderful possibilities that lay ahead for Misty in music, and in life.

Unfortunately, Misty's future would wind down a very different path.

I went back to work when Misty was sixteen, finding a job at Remuda Ranch, which had been one of Wickenburg's most beautiful and popular dude ranches for many years before it was transitioned into a treatment center for people with eating disorders. I started as an Equine Assistant, working with the horses and teaching patients how to ride and how to overcome their fears and grow in self confidence. Eventually I was promoted to Activities Coordinator, continuing to work with patients, but also doing sessions on the high ropes course, planning and facilitating recreation therapy groups and other fun and therapeutic activities. Because I was spending more time away from home, Misty was asked to help pitch in with the care of her five younger siblings. She took on that challenge with adult-like responsibility, letting it be clearly known to her brothers and sisters that she was the boss. But then there were those not so responsible choices that she would eventually make.

The trouble began with the boy next door. Well, I call him a "boy" but in reality he was already an adult, somewhere in his early twenties, when he entered Misty's orbit. She was only sixteen at the time. From the first days Misty began spending time at the home Brad lived in with his mother, Buddy and I sniffed danger. The scent became stronger the day Misty came home from hanging out with Brad.

"Mom, I got invited to go camping with Brad and his family," she said eagerly. "I'd really like to go. Is that okay?" I could smell the beer on her breath.

"Misty, have you been drinking?" I asked, and when she answered my question with silence, I quickly added, "Are you frigging kidding me? You know we don't allow drinking in our lives. No, you are *not* going camping with those people!"

Alcohol was seeping through our door. All those years that I had vowed to keep it out of our family, and it was suddenly carried inside on the shoulders of my oldest child. The angrier I got, the angrier Misty got. Right from the outset of this new male interest in her life, a mother-daughter pattern of head-butting had begun. Things escalated the day Misty stayed out late after having told us she was going to be at a volleyball game at her high school. The police came to our door with news about this mystery.

"Mrs. Musick, we found your daughter Misty out in the desert with that guy who lives next door," the officer explained. "I'm afraid that, well, they had no clothes on and they were...in the car together. I'm sorry, ma'am, but I thought you would want to know."

"No, no! That couldn't have been daughter. She was at the volleyball game at school," I stammered. "Are you sure?"

Keeping a calm, steady gaze, the officer said, "Yes, we're sure."

When Misty finally got home, I chased her around the kitchen table in a rage, trying to talk some sense into her.

"What are you thinking?" I roared. "He's an adult and you're still an adolescent. You're too young to be with him. And you lied to us!"

"Mom, you don't need to make a big deal out of this," Misty insisted.

Oh, but it was a big deal and it would get much bigger. Buddy and I were wise enough to at least put Misty on birth control while we worked to establish firm boundaries, but Misty just shrugged off our attempts to rein her. One day she bolted from the house and drove off in the cute little red car Buddy had given her on her sixteenth birthday. We discovered her staying with a friend and after we got her back home and realized she would continue disobeying our rules, we took her car keys away.

That didn't stop her. When she left again, it soon became clear that she was hiding out in Brad's home next door, with the mother apparently sucked right into the plot. Since our daughter was still very much a minor, we were able to obtain an injunction to prevent him from seeing Misty. As the stalemate continued, I was doing my grocery shopping one day at the Safeway where Misty was working as a courtesy clerk when I happened to see my daughter in the parking lot having a very intimate conversation—with Brad.

"Stay away from our Daughter!" I shouted, not caring who was watching or listening.

We still couldn't keep them apart. I thought Misty was obeying the rules until I began noticing that she wasn't in her room when it was time for her to get up for school in the morning. It didn't take me long to figure out that she had been sneaking out in the early-morning hours and winding up in Brad's bedroom.

"What do I do now?" I kept asking myself. I could not imagine then that this question would come echoing back to me with far bigger stakes years later. All I knew at that time was that Buddy and I had no instruction booklet on how to deal with Misty's risky behavior. We knew that we couldn't stand back and allow our daughter to be hurt... or to hurt herself. Yet, she was pulling further and further away from us, and she was so strong-willed we were afraid that if things kept going in the same direction, the channel of communication between us would be cut off much longer than we could tolerate. We decided to ease off on the confrontations and ultimatums for awhile.

"We've given you guidance," we said. "Now it's up to you to decide how you want to live your life." As well as giving Misty a chance to figure things out for herself, we thought this would also provide Brad the time and space to grow tired of what he was up to. We let go of the court order to keep him away. With her words, Misty reassured us that we could trust her. With her behavior, she demonstrated that we could not. It was time for a new plan.

"Buddy, maybe I'm just playing devil's advocate here," I began, "but what if we tried a different approach? Instead of using the law to try to keep him away from Misty, what if we remind him that he can use the law to stop us from getting in the way?"

Soon we were sitting down for a little talk with this young man who had been causing so much anxiety in our household. When I called him over while Misty was out, I'm sure he was expecting for me to read him the riot act again. He was in for a big surprise.

"Brad, why don't you marry her?" I said. "If you're man enough to have sex with our daughter, then you're man enough to get married to her."

He looked at me as if I had a Martian's antennae sticking out of my head.

"I'll have to think about that," he said finally.

After a brief period of consideration, he surprised us with his answer: yes! And that's how my first-born child, my precious little girl, wound up getting married at age seventeen. When the judge pulled me aside after the simple legal proceeding, the message he delivered wasn't exactly congratulations and best wishes for a long and happy marriage for your daughter.

"I know the family," he said. "You'll be back here for domestic violence." His words were disturbing, but we continued on with our plans. Brad arrived wearing a white tee shirt and a frown as Buddy led them through their vows in our dining room. We toasted their union with sparkling cider and did our best to feign cheer and congratulations.

They soon found their own place to live. I have an image of visiting Misty when she was alone in the little home she and Brad set up on Washington Street. Our battle lines had softened a bit by then. For better or worse, she was an "adult" living her own life. But as I walked in, Misty welled up in tears. Instinctively, I moved closer to hug her. She accepted my embrace.

"Sweetie, oh Sweetie," I said softly. To myself I said, "This just doesn't feel right. She's still just a teenage girl."

"Mom," she said. "It's lonely. It's just so lonely."

Her son Carlos entered her life when Misty was eighteen, and Brendon was not far behind. I was relieved to see that at least Misty was taking good care of her children. They were always well fed, clean and diapered, and, thank God, I never saw signs of abuse. I did, however, witness plenty of evidence of drinking in the house, along with the verbal mistreatment that so often comes as part of the package. What I didn't pick up on, and would only discover many years later, were the clues pointing to substances other than alcohol in my daughter's home life.

"Mom, we were doing almost every drug you could think of," Misty would admit one day, many years later, when the subject of her drug use had finally been placed on the table for discussion. She was laughing when she confessed. The laundry list from those days most likely included acid, cocaine, meth and various other assorted drugs—except heroin.

Without knowing about this drug use at that time, and believing that Misty's own drinking was not out of control, I mostly tried to be a good Grandma while staying out of the way of her marriage and praying for better days. Besides, I had a job and five kids at home to care for. That had become a greater challenge now that I had begun to see another side to this sweet, small, contained town of Wickenburg where everybody knows everybody. Reality had been seeping through the cracks long before I paid any attention to it.

The first time the subject of marijuana came up in our family, one or two of my older kids told me, "Mom, everybody smokes in this town." What? Marijuana was prevalent in quaint, innocent little Wickenburg? I didn't have to go far to continue my education into the dark underground of the community that had pulled us in from southern California with the promise of offering a safe haven from the evils of the world outside. Many people, even today, cling to the naïve view that drugs are only found in big cities, in private bedrooms, filthy bathrooms and darkened alleyways. The truth that I was beginning to learn is that drugs are often right in front of us; we just don't see them. My kids would tell me that boys and girls they knew were out in the nearby desert taking all kinds of drugs. I didn't go out there to investigate, because I was seeing quite enough evidence right outside my own window.

At one home in our neighborhood, we would watch young people ride up on their mopeds or bicycles, get off and carry a backpack to the door. After standing in the doorway for a moment, with backpack quickly opening and closing, off they'd go. At another home within view, "shoppers" would pull down a driveway to an open window. Again, after the briefest of stops, with a backpack or some other container at the ready, they would vroom off. It was like a drive-through candy store.

I tried to alert the police to these neighborhood drug-dealing operations, but they weren't able to do much except tell me more stories about what was going on around town. Apparently, some drug dealers operated a system of leaving a certain color light on in their house to signal when drugs were available. Lights off, don't bother knocking. Lights on, open for business. They would even utilize Christmas lights to help spread the "good news." One day my spying operation zoomed in on a swarm of police cars circling one of the local hot spots. A drug bust resulted, which was encouraging, but by then I was savvy enough to know that this was just one tiny dot on the vast local drug map.

Meanwhile, my son Michael, then an early teen, had started spending more and more time riding his skateboard all around Wickenburg. The cops seemed to assume that wherever skateboards darted, drugs were naturally along for the ride. I was pretty certain that this was not true for my son and his skateboard-loving friends. Here was a perfect opportunity to practice sticking up for my own kids. For years there had been talk of building some kind of place for the kids to skateboard because they often chose dangerous locations to follow their passion. "Let's just do it," I said.

Joining with fellow skaters and their parents, I helped to create the Wickenburg Skate Club. I showed up for a series of meetings with the parks and recreation commission, the town council and other civic groups, where I would cringe at the opposing voices that insisted a skate park would "bring in more drugs." I was trying to create a safe environment where kids like my son would be staying *away* from drugs. But our voices prevailed and a beautiful, well-developed skate park became a part of Coffinger Park, which had modernized and expanded in many other ways since the day I first saw it and sized it up against what I had known in California. I felt honored to dig a shovel at the ground-breaking ceremony and proudly drove around town in my pickup with my license plate that proclaimed my new identity: ZSK8MOM.

I was so busy with my other kids, including my youngest, Josh, who was only a few years older than Misty's oldest son Carlos that I didn't have much time to assist Misty with baby-sitting. We did our best to make her boys feel special whenever we saw them, while I prayed for their parents. It wasn't a big surprise when Misty told us that she and Brad were separating.

"He's growing a marijuana plant in the backyard," Misty explained. "If he gets caught, I'm not going to lose my children over this."

How ironic, I can say in hindsight, that my daughter left her first husband out of fear of the repercussions of having drugs on the premises. Sometime later, she confided that there was more going on inside that marriage and that she was smart enough to get out before the "trouble" predicted by the judge who married her had progressed any further.

I had to wrestle with my Christian beliefs over the idea of accepting the dissolution of a marriage. Once I found a peace about that, I wanted to do whatever I could to support Misty and her two boys in finding their way. Buddy and I agreed to let them stay with us for awhile until Misty rented a tiny apartment of her own. I helped her obtain a job in the Human Resources department at Remuda Ranch, the eating disorders treatment center where I worked. My heart would swell with pride whenever I visited her office. My daughter was professional, friendly and bubbly, quickly earning the trust and confidence of the staff.

Other positive changes were sprouting up. Misty began attending services at Mount Hope again, ending her personal church blackout. Carlos and Brendon joined her for the services, so I could experience the next generation of Christians in our family. And, the best news of all, she was sober! That precious girl I had known, before all the mother-daughter head-butting, her poor choice in men and her regular drinking (and the drugging I didn't know about yet) had waltzed back into our lives like a burst of fresh air.

With Misty back at church, Pastor Duane and the rest of the leadership team were naturally eager for a return engagement of that voice that melts like butter. Every year our congregation would perform the play *For unto Y'All*, a retelling of the gospel story of the birth of Jesus set in the Old West. The play was a natural fit for Wickenburg, and I always enjoyed playing a singing angel with my white boots and cowboy hat. This time Misty was invited to play the role of Mary, which she eagerly accepted.

"How perfect," I said to myself, imagining her up on stage in that prairie dress. "It's another sign that her life is coming back together. My daughter really is getting a clean start!"

Misty devoted herself to the role of Mary, spending countless hours singing at the piano with Mark, the youth pastor who would be playing the role of Joseph. When the lights went up, and Misty unleashed that beautiful voice, our church community again embraced the girl who had once led its choir to national competition. Noting her performance, especially when she sang "Won't you be my little one tonight" to Jesus, Pastor Duane observed, "Misty really nailed it!"

I was so optimistic about my daughter's future. She was sober, she was going to church again, she was singing, she was simply living a godly life. And that's when the emotional roller-coaster ride of being Misty's mother came hurtling back down.

Apparently, something else was in the air during those long hours of Misty and Mark at the piano. As it turned out, they took their closeness off-stage to Misty's apartment, where her co-star was "consoling" her over her sadness from her failed marriage. Suddenly, our little church was rocked by a full-blown scandal. Because Misty was only separated from her husband, she was very much still married in the eyes of the church. And as youth pastor, Mark carried an important and visible responsibility. Many members of our congregation communicated a message that said, "You were teaching our children to be chaste until marriage, and there you were having a fling with a married woman." Some chose not speak to Misty and Mark at all.

When the curtain came down on this little passion play, Mark had been removed of his position and Misty and Mark had decided to live together more than an hour away in Prescott Valley. A marriage and the birth of their son Josiah soon followed. Eventually, the whispers and the wagging of tongues at church began to dissipate and Buddy and I found ourselves confronting a new reality: our daughter's path had abruptly changed yet again. Still in her early twenties she was married a second time, with another son to care for, and she would no longer be living nearby. All I could do was pray that this time things would work out. I comforted myself with the reminder that everyone, especially young adults, makes mistakes. It can take awhile to find their way into mature adulthood. Second marriages sometimes flourish in ways that first marriages never could, especially when alcohol had been ruling the roost.

We visited Misty, our new son-in-law and our three adorable grandsons as often as possible. Misty told us they had joined a church up there and that she and Mark were studying the Bible. That was encouraging news. We also noticed from the start that this was a family that knew how to have fun together. Misty's often crazy sense of humor had an influence on Carlos, Brendon and Josiah, that's for sure. Whenever they ate out at a restaurant, they would all wait eagerly for the moment when Mom would begin to stick wet wipes up her nose. "I wish I could squish my whole body with these," she would laugh, and sometimes she would blow one of the wipes high up into the air. When autumn came, Misty delighted in sticking leaves behind her ears, which of course all the boys had to do too. At home, her sons' favorite reading material was a book titled *The Ghastly Pass*, which presented a simple, scientific explanation of how the human body functions and how we create gas. To boys young and not so young, it was a reason to explode into uproarious laughter every time they heard Misty read the "farting" book.

Misty and Mark took the boys on fun vacations when they could afford it. They loved to tell the story of their visit to Disneyland when Josiah was two. While Misty, Mark and Carlos were riding a roller-coaster at California Adventure Park, the younger boys stayed below with an adult friend. For some reason, Josiah decided it would be great fun to take off both his shoes and throw them into the lake. In the mad rush to find replacement shoes, all they could find were a pair of crocs several sizes too big for him. Josiah adored those crocs so much he wouldn't wear anything else for years.

The boys loved the water, so Mark showed them practically every creek he had known while growing up in Arizona. One favorite spot was Fossil Creek, where the water flowing down from the mountains up north near Flagstaff was icy cold. While nature enthusiasts admired the clear water that enabled waders to view fish and turtles down to the bottom, Misty's sons were more excited by the chance to leap off the six-foot high rock into the freezing water. They also made regular pilgrimages to Grasshopper Point in Sedona, with its tiny sandy beach area that was considered prime real estate for early arrivals. Again, Carlos, Brendon and Josiah were drawn more to the graduated cliffs that loomed as high as sixty feet up. None of them dared to try diving off the top cliff, settling for lesser elevations, but it was always fun to boast about who was going to be the first to take the big plunge.

As Christmas approached one year, Misty informed us that she wanted to host a big meal for both our family and Mark's family. She created attractive individual place cards and laid out her gold-trim china. The meal began with butternut squash soup, progressed to pork tenderloin and vegetables, and was capped by pumpkin pie and other yummy, homemade desserts. "This is our way of giving thanks for our families," Misty announced.

That was one night when I could just sit back and enjoy riding one of the crests of the roller-coaster. My daughter had really grown up, and she was showing her great capacity to love. She also had built on her Human Resources work at Remuda by obtaining a position as Human Resources Director at a physical rehab hospital in her new community. Once again, Misty was popular with her co-workers. She organized costume parties at Halloween, she created Hawaiian luaus, and she would take her candy cart around to staff offices just to bring out a smile on a long or difficult day. Once a year she put together a chili cook-off, which she won just about every time until her best friend Hailey managed to take the crown one year. "I had to stay up all night to come up with the chili that could kick her butt," Hailey laughed. "Everyone at work loved Misty. I spent many fun times at her house, riding four-wheelers and doing kick-boxing with her boys. When I got married in Maine, she and Mark were in our wedding."

Misty even went back to school. When she earned her GED a couple of years after dropping out of high school, she scored at or above the 94th percentile in writing, social studies, science, literature and the arts. Then, after taking beginning courses at her local college, she set

48

her sights on a nursing degree. My daughter had plans and the passion and drive to go after them!

Misty's life track appeared so solid that Buddy and I did not object when Janelle chose to live with Misty and her family while she was sorting out her own education and career choices. It was a long time since Misty had served as something of a baby-sitter for Janelle and her other siblings, but Janelle still looked up to her big sister. In exchange for a place to stay, Janelle helped with childcare while Misty and Mark worked and Misty attended classes. Janelle shuttled the boys to karate classes and soccer practice, spent hours helping them with their homework and was even brave enough to venture inside the boys' bathroom to clean. Janelle would tell me that Misty and Mark spent lots of money, taking the whole family and sometimes even friends out to dinner three or four times a week. I just attributed that to Misty's desire growing up to live more like her long-time piano teacher, Mrs. Edison, who had a much larger and better furnished home than ours. She wanted to live better than her parents, no harm in that.

After Janelle had established herself at Misty's home, Shannon felt the same pull to move in with her big sister while doing on line classes. "I slept on their couch and had just one box of clothes that Misty let me keep in their living room closet," she recalls. "Every morning I would wake up with the boys on my lap."

There was only one thing wrong with this apparently perfect picture of Misty's life as devoted wife, mother, big sister and human resources professional. Misty was drinking—a lot. Apparently, Mark and Misty had begun partying early in their relationship. Alcohol wasn't preventing Misty from juggling her many responsibilities, at least in the beginning, but her sisters had day-to-day evidence of the influence it was beginning to wield.

"When I first moved in she would just have one or two beers a night," Shannon remembers. "But soon she began coming home with a 40, which she had opened in the car. Then it was a six-pack, and later a twelve-pack."

As Janelle remembered it, "Misty would keep drinking late into the night and then usually wind up falling asleep on the living room floor. I really didn't make too much out of it at first. I was a pretty naïve kid, and she remained so high functioning. She was always the life of the party."

Soon Janelle began experiencing what so many loved ones of alcoholics and drug addicts encounter: the need to step in and assume responsibility when the drinker does not do so. After she noticed Misty showing no concern over driving the boy's home after drinking for hours when they were out together, Janelle would insist on staying around to make sure that *she* would be the one to take the wheel. Sometimes she would be stuck waiting for hours to ensure that Misty's three sons would get a safe ride home. What a position to be put in: having to make sure that her big sister didn't drive her own children while drunk!

One night, Janelle and Shannon both witnessed an even scarier sight.

"I was working nights at my job at the local movie theater, so it was about midnight when I was driving home," Shannon explains. "As I approached the driveway I could see Misty and her friend on the sidewalk outside the home with a bottle of whiskey. When Misty saw my headlights, she turned to run away but fell flat on her face. She just face-planted. I think she broke her cheekbone, although she didn't get treated for it."

Janelle remembers talking to Misty the next morning. "She was crying and saying 'I'm so stupid. I don't even know what happened.' That was the first time I really understood that Misty had a problem. After that, I think she might have quit drinking, but that probably lasted about a week until she was right back at it. You couldn't talk to her about it because Misty was very good at making you believe that her problems were not problems."

Misty's problems were just beginning. She lost that great job at the rehab hospital. I can't say for sure that her drinking had caused her dismissal because Misty would get defensive when trying to explain it, admitting only that she "made a few errors" in record keeping. I found out much later that one of those errors was hiring a job candidate before her drug test had passed.

With Misty's drinking habit spiraling, she couldn't hide it from me. I knew that she and Mark were hosting crazy parties where everyone got smashed. On one of my visits there I noticed that she was keeping an ample supply of beer in her fridge, with bottles of hard alcohol up above. "Oh dear God," I said to myself, "are my grandchildren going to have to live like I did growing up around this stuff?" Then, when she and her family would visit us in Wickenburg, it became clear that Misty was losing any ability to have fun without booze. In the middle of our family gatherings she would excuse herself and head out to the store to get her bottle to drink somewhere on the way home, or sneak off to a neighbor's to have a beer or smoke some weed.

I have to admit there were times when I saw her drive off with her children while obviously drunk. If I could turn back the clock, I would have wrestled the car keys from her and said very firmly, "You get a taxi" or "You're staying right here until you sober up." Instead, I just bit my tongue and prayed for their safety. Misty was so strong-minded and masterful at steam-rolling us with her defenses. "You can't tell me what to do, I'm an adult!" she would say.

At least I set boundaries with her when she crossed a line during one Thanksgiving weekend. Our whole family had come together and I was really looking forward to enjoying the company of Misty, Mark and the boys at our home with no alcohol getting in the way. Everything was fine until I walked into the kitchen and found Misty casually pulling a blender from one of my cabinets. On the counter I spotted an open bottle of tequila and some kind of drink mix.

"Excuse me, what are you doing?" I asked.

"Mom, I'm just making margaritas for me and my sisters. It's the holidays!" she said with a defiant smile.

"No! You're not using my blender to put alcohol in!" I roared. "I've told you before, no booze in my house. Take that stuff out of here now!"

Misty backed down, and in a calmer moment later during the holiday gathering she was willing to listen to what I had to say.

"You disrespected me when you tried to bring alcohol in my house," I began. "You know how important this is to me. I've told you many times before; I had enough traumas from alcohol in my life. It ruined my childhood and now you're drinking and I hate it, hate it with every ounce of my being. You have to make your own choices but I don't want my grandchildren to grow up the way I grew up. They've already been through enough."

"Oh Mom, Mom," she said with that familiar grin. And she didn't say anything more. My words, my warnings, my plea was just something she needed to deflect, like a spider crawling up her leg.

That didn't keep me from trying again. I remember another talk, on her turf, at a quieter moment. That time I took the less confrontational, more supportive approach.

"Sweetie, I just hope that you remember that I was raised in an alcoholic home, and that alcoholism runs through our family," I said. "When I see you messing with alcohol, it scares me. Have you thought about going to AA, or getting some kind of help?"

"I'm fine, Mom," she replied in the same calm tone she would use when we were discussing her choice of colors for her curtains. "I'm not going to AA, and I'm not going to therapy. Yes, I drink. It's just something I like to do. Remember when I was first pregnant with Carlos and Brendon, and I told you how I wanted and needed beer during those times? My drinking is not a problem, and this is the last time I'm going to talk about it."

At that moment and the few other times I would dare to bring it up, I decided for better or worse not to take the subject any further. I was always afraid that if I pushed her more, I would be pushing her away from me. And I so badly wanted to keep my daughter in my life, and to have my grandkids around as much as I possibly could. Now I was the one who felt boxed in.

Once, I employed a different strategy. I pulled Mark aside and made my case to him.

"Misty's drinking is serious to me," I said. "It's not a game. Alcoholism runs in my family. I know she won't listen to me, but I'm really afraid that this could get worse and worse over time. Could you at least try setting some boundaries with her? Or maybe you two could go to some kind of counseling together, just to talk about what's happening and hear a professional's point of view?"

Mark politely shook his head. "Mom," he said, using that term I urged all of my sons-in-law or daughters-in-law to address me, "I have talked to Misty about how much she's drinking. I've tried to convince her to slow down. But she won't listen to me either."

The only result of this meeting was getting yelled at by Misty for going behind her back to talk to her husband. I was smart enough not to try to butt in on their marriage after that, but it was so painful to just sit back and watch and wait and hope and pray. The DUIs began to come, but Misty somehow managed to keep landing on her feet. After floundering for awhile in the wake of being fired from her HR job, when she had to re-think her future, she committed to a training program to become a hospital ER technician and forged ahead with her studies in nursing school. She really did appear to be a high-functioning alcoholic, and at times she even displayed a surprising degree of awareness about how she was living. During an email exchange with one of her sisters, Misty responded to a shared exercise that asked a series of questions about the meaning of family and how a family functions together.

"I constantly feel like I'm not a good enough role model for my children," Misty wrote. "But I'm honest with my children about that fact. I often tell them to listen to my advice rather than emulate my behavior."

I spent many hours at home worrying about what Misty was doing, and I suffered through many tense moments around her when I knew she had been drinking or feared that she would soon reach for the bottle. But we had happier, more peaceful times too. Like that day Misty called me to extend a surprise invitation.

"Mom, I know how much you love horses," she began. "Well, I've got a friend who has horses and she told me we could go out riding for a whole day with her. Do you want to come up sometime and ride horses together?"

"Seriously?" I said. "That sounds wonderful. Where?"

"I think she said it was somewhere along the Verde River."

Misty may not have known it, but it had always been a dream of mine to ride a horse in water. When I had my horse as a girl in California, I never had the opportunity to do that. Now my daughter was offering to help me make that old dream a reality. And this would be something new for us. Misty didn't grow up around horses like I did and never seemed to have the burning desire to spend time with this beautiful animal. When I worked with horses at Remuda Ranch, I let her ride one once or twice around the pen. But she never really experienced the freedom that comes with riding a horse out in nature.

"How soon can I come?" I gushed.

It was a warm spring morning, with the sun shining bright, when Misty and I drove to her friend's house. We packed up four horses (the friend's son was also joining us) and all the saddle bags and headed out to the "Dirty Verde." At the trailhead, we unloaded the horses and began to saddle up. Misty tried to get the bridle on her horse by herself, and when I noticed that she lacked the talent and experience to do it, I offered to help.

"No, Mom," she said, "and if I need help, I'll ask her."

This was one time that I could just smile and accept this show of stubbornness—it was simply Misty being Misty. I was the mom and it was my place to back off. I was not going to let anything spoil this day.

When we reached the river, we pulled the saddles and bridles off the horses. That was a safe move because horses will stay with the herd as long as the leader remains in place. Before I knew it, Misty and I were on our horses in the water, just riding.

We rode and we rode and the day became more and more beautiful as it wore on. Misty wasn't an experienced rider but, as always, she was bold and determined to keep up. I didn't say a word to redirect her, even when I was convinced she was on the verge of falling. At one point she was trying to hold her horse's tail and allow the horse to pull her through the water. Well, that was okay until the horse suddenly pooped. Instantly there were all those lovely green road apples floating all around her. Misty just laughed. The sober Misty was always so much fun, and on this day she was absolutely sober.

I didn't want that day to end. Misty and I didn't say much out along the river because we didn't need to. Her gift of sharing this experience with me said it all. Even on the ride back we spoke only briefly, laughing together at some of Misty's attempts to master the art of riding a horse with almost zero experience. As far as I was concerned, she passed the test all aces.

Heading back to Wickenburg alone, I wasn't kidding myself that some corner had been turned, that all the days ahead with Misty would come wrapped in golden sunshine and playful laughter, sharing the natural joys that life can offer when we are open to receive them. I wasn't so naïve as to believe that no more dangers were lurking on the trail ahead. But I was certain of one thing: no matter what the future would bring, I would always remember and forever cherish the day I got to ride horses along the water with my beloved Misty.

CHAPTER 4

Demons & Ditches

MISTY'S APARTMENT WAS a mess. The refrigerator, almost empty of eatable food, was filled with old leftovers and something rotting in the vegetable drawer. Piles of dirty laundry were strewn here and there. The smell of dog poop lingered from the spot behind Misty and Mark's sofa where it had been left for days. Assorted toys, books and other objects necessitated a zigzag pattern of walking along the floors and hallways.

I was answering a distress call from Misty late 2012 and had come to help clean things up. Misty was making her final push toward obtaining her nursing degree at Yavapai College, and while she juggled studying for exams with her full-time job as an ER tech, not to mention her kick-boxing classes, there wasn't much time to keep house. Janelle and Shannon were long gone as helpers since Misty and Mark had been forced to leave their nicer home for this smaller apartment after Misty lost her well-paying job in human resources. Besides, Misty's sisters were now living more independent lives that included boyfriends or husbands. Mark was busy with his job as a paramedic. Misty was carrying a pretty hefty load as she zeroed in on a nursing license, the first big prize on her way toward achieving even greater career goals, and I was more than willing to support her. So I rolled up my sleeves and got busy. After scrubbing out the fridge, I sat down and made out a chore list, making sure to attach the names of Carlos, Brendon and Josiah to many basic duties.

"First, you need to start cleaning up after yourselves. Quit leaving stuff all over the floor," I instructed them. "And guys, you know you're old enough to do your own laundry now too. Just keeping your own laundry basket in your room, and using it, that would be a great start."

The boys didn't argue. They trusted me and knew that I was only trying to help them help their mother get through this challenging time. Anyway, they had gotten used to figuring things out by themselves. Even when Mom was around, she wasn't really "there."

While staying over in their apartment for a few days on this clean-up intervention, I got to see first-hand what I had been hearing from other eyewitnesses in the Musick family. I watched with my jaw dropped open the day the boys came home from school when Misty was at home and didn't even acknowledge them. No "how was your day?" or "do you need help with your homework?" No hugs, no fingers ruffled in their hair, none of the little jokes that they used to hear from their fun and bubbly mom. She just ignored them, poured her drink, went off to the patio and read her books. They weren't even nursing textbooks. Misty had gravitated toward a series of novels that she claimed was her only means of escaping from the pressure to pass her exams.

The real truth was that Misty was as much of a mess as the home she lived in. And the question was whether her mom had the tools and supplies to help get her life back on track. Well, I was certainly ready and willing to get in there and work on it, and I wasn't going to worry about how "soiled" I might get in the operation.

"Sweetie, I'm concerned about you," I said as we sat on her brown sofa. "You're exhausted, you're working so hard all the time, the kids are left to themselves, and obviously you're drinking...Well, I know you don't like me bringing that up. I was really just wondering if there's something else going on for you. You know, like things from your past."

With those words, Misty bolted to a more upright posture on the sofa, where she had been slumped in a corner. She fingered one arm of the furniture as she spoke.

"The past is the past, Mom," she said. "Why would I bring that up now?"

"Well, I just thought that if there was anything that your dad or I had done that would be helpful for you to talk about. I mean, we certainly weren't perfect parents and...."

When I saw the tears begin to well up on her face, I knew it was time to put on my internal silencer.

"Okay, I'll tell you what I remember from the past," Misty sputtered. "You remember that day in church after what happened with Andy, and Dad putting that stupid ring on my finger with all those people watching us at the altar, and the guy pointing his finger and telling me I was going to hell?"

As hard as I tried, I could never erase those tapes from my mind. They came rushing forward now, in full color and vivid detail. *We were so wrong that day, and now look at how badly she has been hurt. Did our actions contribute to her drinking habit?*

"Yes, I do remember that day," I sighed.

"Do you think I felt good about losing my virginity in an outhouse? Do you!?" Misty muttered.

Fighting back my own tears, I managed to say, "We made a terrible mistake. We should never have put you in a position where all those people in church were judging you and—"

"Mom, you were always judging me! I felt like I could never be good enough for you. But I was a good girl, I really was!"

My breathing quickened. It felt like my heart was breaking.

"And do you remember the prom?" Misty went on. "*All* my friends were going but you wouldn't let me go! I felt like a freak. You just made me go on that 'date night' with the youth pastor with all the other girls from church who weren't allowed to go to the prom. Do you think I liked that?"

I hadn't thought about that prom for years, but those memories also came pouring back to me. "Unless you're dancing with your spouse, secular dancing was sinful," the people at Mount Hope had believed. A high school prom was just not a "godly environment" and no good Christian girl should ever be allowed to go. At the time, I figured if that was what my church was saying, it must be right. "You can't go. The prom is full of temptations," I had told Misty back then. And yet, how many proms did I get to attend when I was a teenage girl?

Now, fighting back tears, my stomach churned. *Dear God, what did we do back then? Faith should never be so rigid, so fear-based. Why did we do this to our precious daughter?*

"Misty, I am so sorry," I finally said out loud. "I wish there was a prom today. I would definitely let you go. You missed out and I feel so badly about that."

Her crying briefly slowed to muffled sobs.

"Can I give you a hug?" I asked.

"No, Mom, not yet," she responded firmly. A minute later she reached into her bag of childhood wounds and pulled out another story or two. I tried to just listen patiently and empathetically, but Misty didn't unveil any more big surprises. The real surprise was that she was talking about all these painful experiences at all. With her life-of-the-party personality, this was not her usual style.

Of course, her complaints got my wheels spinning. I had sometimes worried that holding onto all that unresolved childhood pain and regret could have had something to do with Misty's heavy drinking. Maybe it wasn't too late to do something about that.

"Sweetie, if there's anything that your dad and I can do to help you deal with all these things from the past, we will make ourselves available," I began. "Maybe if you had a therapist to talk to, it would be easier to say everything you need to say."

I wanted to take her silence that greeted my suggestion as a sign that she might actually consider seeking professional help. If only she could open up about what was really bothering her, maybe the key could be unlocked to the door of sobriety. Well, a mother has to have hope.

The truth was that major influences from the present were also contributing to my daughter's troubled state. Janelle was the first one to catch wind of that during a small pre-Christmas family gathering at her home. Noticing that Misty looked sad and bedraggled, Janelle pulled her aside.

"Are you okay?" she asked Misty. "I'm your sister, remember. If you need to talk about something, you can always talk to me." The next morning Misty invited Janelle over to her apartment. She found Misty in bed, crying.

"I'm just feeling so guilty," Misty said, and she slowly revealed why: she had been having an affair with a young man she met in nursing school. Apparently they began to get chummy while riding to class together. And it was all happening while this guy's wife was suffering from cancer. While Janelle tried to absorb this jolting news, Misty added words that stung Janelle to the core: "I don't want to take care of Mark anymore, and I really don't even want to be a mom anymore."

Janelle had spent hours and hours caring for those three boys. Her bonds with Carlos, Brendon and Josiah were as deep as any she had in her life. Now Misty wanted to walk away from them. "All my life I had looked up to Misty as my big sister, but at that moment it stopped," Janelle explained. "If she was going to act like that, she couldn't be my hero anymore."

Even with fire alarms sounding all around her head, Janelle held her tongue while Misty continued to vent about her life. After Misty left, Janelle reluctantly stayed true to her sister's request not to tell anyone about the affair. Mark soon found out from the wife of the other man anyway, and he and Misty sat down to try to dismantle the time bomb ticking in their marriage. Words were passed, promises were made. Misty insisted that her intimate relationship with this guy, Rick, was over. In an email to a friend, she admitted that "Mark and I have had a bad year, but we're working it out. God, it's not easy."

By the night of Misty's graduation in December, I wasn't thinking about Misty's affair. Hopefully this was a situation where the past *was* just the past. My daughter was becoming a nurse, and it was time for our family to celebrate!

When Buddy and I and the rest of our family arrived at the ceremony, we found Mark already seated and filed into his row. We watched intently and when the moment for Misty to receive her diploma approached, we were ready to snap our photos and raise our arms in triumph. Except that the second our daughter's name was announced, the man seated directly behind me screamed loudly, "Misty! Misty!!" I happened to gaze over at Mark and saw him turn behind him with an icy glare. As I soon found out, this was that guy Rick. At this special moment for Misty, he was behaving as if he were a part of our family.

When the ceremony ended and the nursing graduates huddled with their loved ones, Misty kept her distance from Mark. She stayed mostly with her friends, and that guy appeared to be part of the group. "She's acting so strangely, kind of hyper" I said to Buddy at one point. She was also ignoring her three boys. A night that was supposed to be celebratory was rapidly turning sad.

Misty's post-graduation plan was for everyone to gather at a restaurant in Prescott, but the directions she tried to give us by phone from her car made no sense. When Buddy finally figured things out well enough to find the place, it was soon clear that Misty again was going to choose to sit and talk with her friends, not her husband, her sons and the rest of our family. I felt deflated. Why would my daughter not want to spend time with her family during this big occasion? We all loved her, we had all been rooting for her to make it, and we all welcomed this important step in her life.

When the caravan of family and friends made its way to Misty and Mark's apartment, Buddy and I quickly said goodbye. Apparently, the celebration was going to continue at a nightclub where there would be lots of drinking going on. I had no interest in being a part of that scene, and of course we were not invited. At least Mark and Misty were going together. On the ride back down the mountain to Wickenburg, Buddy and I tried to make sense of Misty's behavior.

"I don't like it, don't like any of it," I said. "But Misty's an adult. She's going to have to figure this out by herself."

First thing the next morning, I got a call from Mark.

"Mom, are you sitting down?" he asked.

"Oh my gosh, Mark, what is it?" I said, my voice rising.

"I left Misty in the bar last night because I hit...that guy. I decked him, Mom."

"You did what? What happened?"

As Mark described it, Rick apparently arrived at the club already drunk. One of the first things he did was slap Misty on the butt—right in front of Mark.

"Mom, I'm not the type of person to do things like that," Mark said of his reflex response. He didn't have to reassure me. I knew that my son-in-law was a gentle man.

"No, but he dishonored you, and you took your honor back," I shot back. "I would have hit him too."

Misty chose to stand by her boyfriend's side in all of this, and in a matter of days she had left her home with Mark and her children and moved in with Rick. His wife had died of cancer by then and, with a little bit of family help and lots of child care, he was single-parenting two toddlers. So my daughter who had declared that she was tired of parenting was going to live in a home with two kids younger than her own three sons.

That's not all she was bringing into her life. We soon heard that during his wife's health decline Rick had been taking her pain medication and was no doubt still using dangerous and addictive drugs. With a promising future as a nurse about to begin, and the love of her family behind her, this is what our beloved Misty was choosing.

Though I had vowed to Buddy that I wouldn't butt in, I couldn't hold back from trying to get answers. I really didn't believe that I could do anything to stop Misty, but I just wanted to make some sense out of this craziness. So I asked, as respectfully as I could manage: why?

"Mom, I just need to take a break right now," she explained, and I knew she meant not only from her marriage but her mothering of her own three kids. "I was so young when I got married the first time, and

I was still young when I went off with Mark. This time I just feel like I'm the one choosing, like I'm finally free."

"Well, being young is not an excuse for your actions," I said. "And, it seems like you had a good marriage with Mark. I just don't understand."

"But I never had a man that I really loved before," she said. "Now I do."

This sure didn't sound like love to me. There was a lot more I could say about what it *did* look and sound like, but mostly I refrained. I tried to listen while Misty complained about Mark, running through what sounded to me like the usual frustrations of sorting out married life together.

"Why don't you two go to marital therapy?" I suggested. "Your dad and I tried to teach you how to hang on and work things through when you're having hard times in marriage."

"But Mom, I love Rick," she said again, and from there I knew that all I could do was pray for her. There was no arguing with Misty, and I could tell that this path she had chosen was one that she was not going to leave behind unless and until she believed a better one was available.

I also knew enough about separation and divorce to understand that the kids suffer the most. Carlos and Brendon were thrust into choosing between spending most of their time with their mother at her boyfriend's home or staying primarily with Mark, their step-father. Carlos's connection with his mom was so strong that he wanted to stay with her whenever he could, even though being at Misty and Rick's home meant that he would be expected to look after Rick's two young kids. Carlos was all of thirteen years old. The only time he was free of the responsibility of taking care of two little kids were the seven hours he spent at school. Otherwise, he accepted a routine of making their breakfast before they were whisked to child-care and then watching over them, entertaining them, sometimes even changing them when he was home. Rick was still in nursing school and Misty had managed to obtain work as a hospice nurse, but even when they weren't busy with those responsibilities the two adults of this household weren't doing much supervising of the two and three year old toddlers under their roof. They were too busy partying.

One night Misty and Rick invited Shannon along on one of their binges. The plan was to hit the restaurants and bars in a notorious night-life section of Tempe. Because Shannon was not yet twenty-one, Misty gave her sister her own ID and a backup insurance card to get her through the door. "Misty hardly ate during dinner," Shannon recalled, "and that was very weird for me to see because Misty was always a big foodie." It turned out that the weird behavior was just beginning. Rick, who was drinking heavily, kept getting up and leaving the table every twenty minutes. After awhile, Misty began disappearing too, leaving Shannon alone in her first night in a bar. Soon after Shannon's boyfriend Brent arrived as planned to join the party, Misty and Rick got up to leave. "We're going back to our hotel," Misty announced.

Although annoyed and confused by what happened at the bar, Shannon and Brent agreed to meet Misty and her boyfriend for breakfast the next morning. Misty was looking haggard and was not shy about revealing what had kept her up most of the night.

"They hired an SUV with a driver and stopped at a bunch of clubs, where they partied and threw money at strippers," Shannon reported. "When she explained about how the driver pulled over so they could 'have fun back there,' I told her she was gross and I didn't want to hear anymore. She was so excited to be telling me all this and bragging about how much fun they were having spending the money from Rick's wife's life insurance."

While Misty continued to flaunt this new lifestyle and the man in the middle of it, I worried about the toll this was having on my grandsons. I did whatever I could to help Mark hold things together for those boys. Fortunately, a kind and caring school counselor was devoting hours to assisting Carlos in carrying the weight of seeing his parents separated and his mother living a life she mostly tried to hide from him while he was with her. I was already angry with Rick for his role in causing division within our family, and then he tried to raise the stakes higher. He actually had the nerve to suggest that Buddy and I start treating *him* as our son-in-law and boot Mark out of our lives.

Those were the storm clouds already rising in April when the eighth birthday of Misty and Mark's son Josiah drew near. When Misty called us to discuss her plans, she made it clear that she and Rick were drawing a line in the sand. The big family birthday party would be at her new home with Rick—there would be no party at Mark's house.

"I'm your daughter," she argued. "You have to come to our party here."

When I heard those words, I took out my own stick and immediately set out to re-draw the lines.

"If you two are inviting us, we will go to your party," I said. "But I am not going to stay away from Mark's house for Josiah's birthday. If that means we have two birthday parties, so be it."

The message I was sending to Misty and especially to her boyfriend was this: you are not going to make me stop loving my son-in-law!

So I enjoyed the birthday party for Josiah at Mark's house and a day or two later our whole family headed for the public park where Misty had planned the party that she and Rick would host. We were all there on time but there was no sign of Misty and Rick, nor was there any sign of Josiah, Brendon and Carlos. This was disturbing because one thing about Misty was that she was always on time, even when she had been partying. When she asked us to pick up the boys and bring them to the park, we did what we were told without making a fuss. In my mind, there had already been enough arguing about this event. Still, when they kept us waiting at the park even longer, the party mood was rapidly fading.

Finally, Misty and Rick showed up. We were anticipating a fun and lively gathering with lots to eat, because Misty was known for going all out on quality and quantity of food. Since we were outside, we assumed that we would be treated to a barbecue. But when Misty and Rick arrived, we noticed they had purchased a small number of cup-cakes and a tiny birthday cake that would barely feed the kids. Then Misty set about introducing Rick to all of us. Buddy and I had yet to meet this young man face to face.

"Lord, let me be Christ-like right now," I said to myself. "I don't agree with any of this, but I seek to be loving and accepting."

I have to admit that over those next several minutes I struggled at living up to my ideals. Buddy and I, and most of my kids and their spouses or significant others, were doing our best to be kind to Rick. In response, he avoided us. He didn't make eye contact with any of us, and his answers to our carefully worded questions were brief.

Although my anger was threatening to surge to the surface over Rick, my attention soon shifted to the sight of my daughter. She was so thin! I had always known Misty to be curvy, but now it was like she had just gone through some kind of shrinking machine. At that time I was still too naïve to recognize what was really operating the controls of that machine.

"Misty, you've lost so much weight. You must be doing a lot of yoga," I said.

"No, not really," she said with a faint grin.

"Well, Sweetie, are you eating enough?" I responded, and she immediately changed the subject.

As soon as Josiah finished unwrapping his presents, Misty and Rick began to wrap up the party. This was a party that Buddy and I and Misty's siblings had driven an hour or longer to attend.

"Gosh, Sweetie, is that it?" I said after I pulled her aside. "Aren't we going to your house or anything?"

"Oh, well, let me talk to Rick," she said.

After a quick consult, they informed us that we could visit them at their house for awhile, but that we would have to go to Janelle's house nearby to wait until they had a chance to clean up. Again we entertained the boys and tried not to draw more attention to what we all sensed was strange behavior. When they finally told us it was "safe to come" and we arrived at their home, we were met with a firm announcement.

"This is our bedroom—no one goes in there," Misty said as she pointed to a room at the entry. "There's also a bathroom in there. Nobody uses our bathroom either."

The light bulb in my mind was still not going on. I was taken aback by their need for such strict boundaries, but it was their home. We would abide by the rules that Misty and Rick were laying out.

More signs that *something* was going on kept showing up. I noticed how Misty and Rick made it a point to place the key to their bedroom in the door frame high above the door, well out of reach of Rick's two children. Then we all could see that Rick was spending more than half his time inside that forbidden bedroom. I teased, "We haven't seen much of Rick, and I hope we're not scaring him."

"I'm not scared of any of you," he announced with an icy glare during one of his rare moments in the living room. Then he quickly shifted his gaze back to his computer. I had never been treated with such disrespect by any of my sons-in-law or daughters' boyfriends. It was almost impossible imagining that this man would ever really be part of our family. I was so stung by his words that I wasn't even thinking about what else could explain all this bizarre behavior.

Misty managed to scrounge together a quick meal for our little "party," which, other than the kids frolicking around had been getting quieter and more strained by the minute. When Rick's two little ones began acting up, it was Misty, not their father, who intervened.

"Get over here!" she shouted. As they immediately came to her and stood at attention, I was almost waiting for them to salute. Suddenly I felt sad and frightened for them. Carlos, Brandon and Josiah were not the only children suffering from what was happening in my daughter's life.

So the party ended as awkwardly as it had begun, and we all drove off trying to make sense of what we had just witnessed. Buddy and I swapped references to all those strange scenes and interactions. "She just looked really bad, like she's sick," Buddy said. But we weren't getting very far in putting the pieces of the puzzle together.

Brian and his wife Heather, as I would soon learn, were a step or two ahead of us. Heather had grown up in a family of drug addicts and her father was still abusing crystal meth. While they were at Rick's home during the strange family scene, Heather had been observing the signs and bringing them up to Brian.

"I think Misty's doing drugs," she whispered to Brian at one point.

"Really? How do you know that?" he asked.

"Look at the way they keep hopping up from their chair every two seconds," she said. "That's a sign of meth. And closing off the bedroom to us, that's another sign that something is going on in there that they need to keep hidden—like their drugs."

Heather also noticed that Rick was not the only one retreating to the private bedroom. Misty also was disappearing behind the locked door, and Heather observed that you could almost set a timer to her visits back there, every twenty to thirty minutes.

"That's not a meth thing, more like cocaine or something like that," Heather reported. Though she no longer needed to whisper because moments would pass without Misty or Rick in the room, she still kept her voice down. "When she comes out, watch for the halo where the white powder has been around her nose," she added. Sure enough, Heather and Brian both detected the halo. Misty, whom all of us knew to be a high-functioning drinker, had moved on to the world of drugs.

When Brian and Heather shared their suspicions with me, I didn't want to believe them. My first-born daughter was using drugs? I trusted Heather's knowledge and judgment, but I was not ready to fully accept the evidence until it was confirmed by another source. Within a few days I once again heard that strong, yet whispered voice in my head.

"Misty, what you are involved with will strongly affect your health and your wealth."

I tried to reason away the voice, but the message kept coming back to me, *"It will strongly affect your health and your wealth."* That's when I knew that my daughter was dabbling in drugs, and that it wasn't a recreational practice. I also knew that it was my obligation as her mother, and a servant of God, to share this message with my Daughter. I called and explained that I had heard the familiar voice once again. I had faith that my daughter still trusted my relationship with the Lord to honor what I had received.

"Mom, what you have heard is true," she admitted after sucking in her breath. "But I can't tell you more right now."

"Sweetie, we're here for you," I said with mist in my eyes. "Please be open with us. I am so worried that what you are doing could destroy your body, your mind, your whole life."

Misty called back a few days later.

"Mom, I'm going to tell you the truth," she said. "I'm shooting up. I'm...hooked on heroin."

HEROIN? I gasped and wrapped my arms over my shoulders. I couldn't speak for a moment; I could barely breathe. I thought the floor would fall from underneath me.

"Are you serious, Misty? Heroin? But what...what are you going to do?" I stammered. Sweetie, people don't just come clean from this. You need to get treatment.

"Mom, I don't want you to worry about this," Misty said firmly. "I don't need your help. I can take care of this in my own way. I just wanted you to know what was happening because I don't like keeping secrets. I will deal with this."

After Buddy's initial shock at hearing the news, we were both coming to the realization that so much of what we had seen made sense now: the strange birthday party in the park, Misty's extreme weight loss, the jumping up and down from their chairs at their house, the secretiveness about their bedroom and bathroom.

"That's where they must be shooting heroin!" I proclaimed. "The drugs and the mess that comes with it must have been all over their apartment, and we were right there."

Buddy reminded me of an earlier episode in which Misty had obtained "pain medication," supposedly for gall stones. At the time, both of us had doubted that she really had the gall stones. What else had she been lying to everyone about? What other secrets might she be keeping? Where was all this going to lead her...and us? The questions crashed together like roaring waves on a California beach, and I was caught in the surf. Alone that night, I sat down and reached out for help.

"Oh dear God, please, please save my daughter!" I pleaded. "Help us find some way to heal all her broken pieces and restore her to health." I kept repeating that heartrending prayer: *Dear God, please save my daughter.*

Feeling calmed enough to begin planning my next steps; I was very clear on what I had to do: share this horrible news with my other five children. I would not keep this devastating information from my family, and they deserved to be free of any further deception on Misty's part. As a family we had already been impacted by Misty's actions, and we were all going to be involved in whatever was going to happen next. Yes, we were all in this together.

Fortunately, Brian, Janelle, Shannon and Josh were all still living in Arizona. Only Michael had moved far away, to Tennessee. Brian and Heather already believed Misty was taking drugs, but even they were shocked that her drug of choice was heroin. "I never even thought to look for needle marks on her arms," noted Heather, and we both realized that Misty had worn short sleeves at the birthday party. It was almost as if she wanted us to figure it out. Janelle and Travis were frightened by the news, since they lived not far from Misty in Prescott Valley. Could the dangerous tentacles of the drug world that Misty had now plunged into reach their doorstep? When I told Brent and Shannon, she shared with me a recent incident in which Misty had asked to borrow her urine to take a mandatory urine analysis for her current work as a hospice worker. Shannon wisely declined. Josh, who was still living at home with us as a teenager, blurted out, "She's being so stupid! This isn't supposed to happen to my sister. She's supposed to be someone I can look up to!" When I called Michael, he was fighting through tears when he responded, "Mom, once they start shooting up, there is usually no turning back."

I cringed when I heard those words, and after doing my best to reassure Michael I scrambled my brain for some way to reassure *me*.

"No, my daughter will not die from heroin!" I said to myself. "She will go to rehab. She will fight this addiction, she will turn away from this deadly road and she will win. Then she will tell her story to help others. I know this is true because I know my daughter."

I could not accept Misty's insistence that she would handle her heroin addiction her own way. I was still working for treatment centers for eating disorders and co-existing conditions such as alcohol and substance abuse. Now at the Rosewood Centers for Eating Disorders in Wickenburg, I understood that if addicts are really serious about getting well they need to seek out support and treatment. That was especially true for heroin addicts. And if Misty was not going to follow the path to a rehab program herself, I would just have to lead her to one myself.

So I surrounded myself with every resource I could locate and hunkered down to begin my investigation. I knew that most drug treatment programs were very expensive, and on the tail end of raising six kids Buddy and I didn't have deep pockets to dip into. But I was soon reassured that I would be guided in the right direction. A contact whom I once worked with at Remuda informed me that his son had opened a treatment center up in Prescott, not far from Misty's town. With his compassionate assistance, I was able to obtain a scholarship to help cover Misty's cost at The Bridges Network. We had a ticket to her recovery and I couldn't wait to give it to her.

"I found a place for you to deal with this problem, and it's free. It's a miracle, Sweetie!" I told her.

"Mom, I didn't say I was ready to go into treatment. There are things I need to take care of. I can't just walk away. And I told you that I would handle this my own way," she said softly, knocking my excitement down about five notches.

"But, what about your boys? They need you to take care of this. Think of them," I said, my voice growing fainter as I tried to continue my reasoned plea.

"Mom, back off," she said after a long pause, and I realized that as sad and frustrating as it was to admit it, I would have to step aside to see what she would do next. As the Bible tells us, there is "a time for every purpose under the heaven." (Ecclesiastes 3:1). With Misty I knew that there were times when I could nudge her, at least a little, and times when I needed to pull back. She already had gotten angry with me for telling her siblings about her heroin addiction and was now expressing her anger to them. "Mom doesn't know what's she's talking about. She's making way too much out of this." Trying to force treatment on her now would only drive her further away from getting the help she desperately needed.

So I gave her the number for Roy Thomas, the director of the rehab program at Bridges Network. I also made sure that Roy had Misty's contact info. Then I tried my best to do what is probably the hardest thing for any mother of a drug addict to do: wait.

While I waited, I questioned myself for practically everything I did or didn't do, said or didn't say, in trying to respond to Misty's addiction. I would cry so hard at night and into the morning that sometimes I would have to call in to excuse myself from work, something I never wanted to do. I was feeling helpless—powerless really. And still I waited.

As the days and weeks dragged by, I did not receive the news that I was praying for, that Misty had decided on her own terms to enter treatment. Instead, I received more of the kind of news that I did *not* want to hear.

Now that I knew that Misty and Rick were using heroin in a home with two young children, I was more concerned for those two kids. They deserved better than a father taking drugs living with a married woman using right along with him. When I wondered about the possibility of some intervention through Child Protective Services, I discovered that CPS already had been alerted to the unhealthy and dangerous situation in Rick's home by someone he knew. How did CPS respond? From what I was told, they informed Rick and Misty that they would come to assess their home situation as a follow-up to this report...in two days. Well, forty-eight hours is more than enough time for drug addicts to sweep all evidence of their habit out of sight and put on a clean and happy face. They passed their test with flying colors, and then went right back to the needle. The solid income Misty was making as a traveling hospice nurse was probably being funneled mostly into drugs, after covering the barest necessities for the kids.

Meanwhile, Carlos was still coming to Misty's place to be near his mom. He told Mark that whatever his mother and boyfriend may have been doing, they kept it hidden from him. One evening Janelle was visiting Mark and the three boys when Misty called her. "Can you babysit Rick's kids while we go out?" Misty asked. Janelle was torn. She had met these two precious children with their cute smiles and wanted to care for and protect them. She also knew that it would not be healthy for her to get caught up in what was happening in that house or to do anything to enable her sister's drug use. Seconds after she told Misty that she was not available, Carlos's phone buzzed. Janelle knew instantly that her sister had simply turned to her teenage son to fulfill her needs for a sitter so she could party on.

Moments like that just tore at all our hearts. Soon after Shannon learned that she was pregnant, she couldn't resist the urge to show her big sister her belly. When Shannon arrived at Misty and Rick's home,

Misty at least pretended to be excited. In reality, she looked terrible and Rick was passed out. One of his kids was climbing all over Shannon seeking attention. She knew that Misty was probably high. "I guess I have to go now," Shannon said and quickly left.

Finally, that August, something happened that not even Misty could hide. Janelle was the first to hear the news when she got a phone call from a woman who was attending school at the campus where Janelle was working. Apparently this woman had known Rick and his wife. "Your sister just got in a car accident right across the street from my house," she told Janelle, "and something's really wrong with her. She's acting kind of crazy. I don't know if she's on something or what." As Janelle sought more details, she learned that Misty had driven Rick's minivan into a ditch and that attempts to reach Rick to inform him were unsuccessful.

"So what I am supposed to do now?" Janelle asked herself. That's when she called me at work.

"Have you heard anything about Misty getting into a car accident?" she asked, prompting me to begin a wild flurry of phone calls. Misty, who refused medical treatment despite obviously suffering injuries, wound up with a DUI. It was not her first. Other charges apparently were pending. When I spoke to her after she had been interrogated, her words were still so slurred I could not understand her. The police officer that I spoke to painted an even darker picture. Misty had been high on meth for three days and, as he described it, "her veins are the worst I've ever seen."

My daughter was falling fast, and with these stains on her record, and the initial CPS report that she had been using drugs, she was in severe danger of losing her nursing license.

That's probably the primary reason that Misty finally picked up the phone and proclaimed to Roy Thomas, "I'm ready for rehab." It wasn't my plea for her to take action for her health and for the future of her three children. It wasn't remorse over all the lies and manipulations, and the many impossible situations that she had been placing her family in. It wasn't an admission that she was powerless over her addiction to heroin, as well as to alcohol and all the other drugs. Misty just wanted to save her career before it was washed down the drain, like the blood that sometimes would flow from sticking needles in her veins.

Buddy and I drove up to Prescott the day Misty was to be admitted to the Bridges Network. After worrying that she would not show up, I was relieved when she arrived with Rick. Apparently they had to "take care of something" before they could come. Misty was high.

"That's typical for addicts going to recovery for the first time," Roy assured me. "The important thing is that she is here. She has a chance to get clean, to get well, and we're going to do everything we can to help her."

As he escorted Buddy and me into the hallway outside his office, I noticed a collage of photos. Glancing more closely, I discovered that this was a memorial to addicts who had died from their addiction. I quickly looked away. Stepping into another summer day when the Arizona temperatures would be rising well above 100 degrees, I understood that Roy Thomas was absolutely right. *The important thing is that she is here.* It didn't matter why Misty finally got herself into a treatment program. I understood that many addicts reached this point while kicking and screaming, showing no immediate signs of wanting to embrace true, long-term recovery, but they still found the courage and strength to turn their lives around. And that was just what was going to happen to my daughter!

I was doing my best to practice what I had been learning about a healthy approach for the loved one of someone hooked on drugs: separate the addict from the person. Misty the addict had fallen into a pattern of horrible, destructive behavior, and she was spreading the harmful influence of her actions to everyone in her wake. Misty the person was still that intelligent, funny, talented, hard-working, goal-driven young woman that I had raised and nurtured. This was a woman capable of being warm and loving, someone who could lift up the spirits of those around her with her presence rather than dragging them down by her actions.

That healthy person was still inside her, and this treatment facility, this experience, was going to help to bring that person out again. As I drove down the mountain to Wickenburg that is what I knew I had to believe.

CHAPTER 5

—— ⚬ ——

The Blood Red Trail

ROY THOMAS UNDERSTOOD the long and difficult road any addict must navigate to accept the need for treatment and then to actually take advantage of the opportunity to get well, to stay clean and sober. He was an addict in recovery himself, and he remembered all his attempts to get clean, how he had failed *eight times* until finally finding his way. He structured the Bridges Network with a long-term commitment in mind, pointing to the encouraging statistics for those able to stick with it beyond the first thirty days and continue on to 100 days of treatment.

From his first talk with Misty, Roy sensed the challenges ahead for her. But he could also envision her potential. Like most people who met Misty, he was struck by her strong presence. "Bright, talented, but also tormented," he noted from his first meeting. He knew the pain she was suffering from wrestling with the demons of drugs, but he could clearly imagine a positive future when she had torn herself loose from their grasp. Checking through her background, he put a big check mark next to the details regarding her health-related education and experience as a nurse.

"The field of drug treatment and recovery could be a perfect fit for you someday," he told Misty. "I can see you working in a drug treatment center, handling the medical detox. You would understand all the health issues involved, and you know what it's like to be caught up in addiction and feel like you can't get out."

Misty smiled at the idea of using her gifts and calling upon her own experiences, both positive and negative, to help other addicts save their lives. Perhaps God really was opening doors for her. The question for Misty, for her helpers at the center, and for all of us who loved her was whether she could do the excruciatingly hard work required for any addict to claim recovery. Could she find the courage to walk through that door? Could she stay the course of rehab and recovery, weathering all the storms that could strike at any time, threatening to wash those positive images away?

Those storm clouds hovering over Misty's head were also encircling others in her life. While I was hopeful that Misty could walk the path of recovery, I also knew that she was in love with a heroin addict. As Buddy and I drove home after checking Misty into Bridges, I started thinking about Rick home alone with those kids, with heroin and other drugs right under their roof. Misty was no longer there to at least try to keep the children safe and healthy, and my grandson Carlos wasn't going to show up anymore without his mom to visit.

"Maybe I should call Rick to see if the kids are okay," I mentioned to Buddy, and when he agreed I quickly dialed Rick's number. No answer. Was he just ignoring me, or was there already trouble? I kept thinking of those children. What would happen to them if their father took too many drugs and didn't have Misty there to try to bring him around? Who would feed them? Who would watch over them? I had to do something!

"There are drugs in that home," I found myself explaining to the police officer who responded to my distress call. "My daughter was taking heroin with her boyfriend there and now she's in treatment. There are babies living there. Someone has to make sure they are alright. Can you do something, maybe some kind of wellness check?"

"We'll see what we can do, ma'am," he said.

"Thank you so much for being willing to protect those children," I said. "And when you go there to check up on them, please make sure that my call is kept confidential."

I didn't like poking into Rick's affairs, but I also understood that for better or worse this young man was very much a part of my daughter's life. And so was that little boy and little girl. I don't know how long it was until I received the text message, but I remember the words: "I know it was you, you bitch." Now I was really in the middle of things, and I couldn't just walk away. I got on the phone with this man who had been muddling in our family's lives for months.

"You had no business calling the police on me!" Rick shouted, using more colorful language than I will share here. "And I take care of my kids. I'm a *good* father."

"You're what? You're an addict! Don't make yourself out to be Father of the Year to me," I growled, the tone of my own voice rising. "You are using drugs with children in that house right now. You're the one who introduced my daughter to the needle and now she's a heroin addict fighting for recovery. You're in no position to be telling *me* what to do!"

Before hanging up, Rick made sure to call me several nasty names. I didn't answer back but wished I could have.

According to the rules at Bridges, Misty was not supposed to have any contact with Rick during treatment. Unfortunately, she found a way around the rules. Apparently she tricked the staff into allowing her to use an electronic device by explaining that it was going to help her connect with her music. She had told them all about her piano playing and her singing, and I'm sure she convinced them that anything they did to support her love of music was going to enhance her efforts to recover. Oh, my daughter could tell a story! And that's how she and Rick kept in touch. I didn't know what they were communicating about, but I knew enough to conclude that they weren't talking about how well Misty's treatment program was progressing and how Rick should follow her into treatment right away.

"I love him," Misty had said to me many times, denying the reality that they she and Rick were poison together. I think she was more in love with the drugs that she shared with him, or maybe she was pulled in by the excitement of being with the "bad boy." Whatever the motivation for coming together, all I knew now was that this man potentially stood in the way of Misty's recovery.

Misty's first slip-up happened not long after she settled into the treatment program. She got caught breaking one of the other rules, and she also had a dirty urine analysis (UA). Roy and his staff decided to give her a second chance. He remembered how he had struggled with recovery, and how each time he would make progress "life would hit me" and he would stumble. They advised Misty to enter a lock-down unit so she could be safe and focus on the work she needed to do, and when she refused, they allowed her to stay with a support person to detox and regain some stability. At home, I was praying that Misty could avoid temptations and focus on what she needed to do to follow the program. It was a see-saw process.

For a time, Misty buckled down and re-committed to her program. She had been allowed back in to the residential units at Bridges, and Roy reported that she seemed happier. At one point she even appropriately communicated with me about her need for boundaries in our relationship—another upswing on the see-saw.

Meanwhile, Misty had instructed me to monitor her Facebook page, presumably so she could be alerted to signs of trouble with her contacts in the drug underworld. That's when I noticed the name of Diane on Misty's Friends' list. Interestingly, she was also Facebook friends with Rick and his late wife. I decided that I would reach out to her to seek any possible new information that could help support Misty. When Diane responded, I discovered that she was Rick's wife's step-mother. As I shared my concerns about the kids living alone with Rick, it was clear that this woman and I were kindred spirits. Over dinner, we brainstormed ways to assist Misty and those two children. Although we didn't come up with any concrete solutions, I felt encouraged to have an ally.

That night, I went home feeling hopeful again. Misty was going to stick with her rehab program this time and the children she had been caring for would be taken care of. Then my cell phone rang. When I saw Mark's number, I was afraid it was about Misty.

"Mom, are you sitting down?" he said. "It's Rick. He...he's dead."

"What? Are you sure?" I stammered, and Mark reminded me that as a paramedic he knew almost everyone in law enforcement in the Prescott Valley area.

"Was it an overdose?" I asked.

"Yes, it appears to be an overdose."

Just like that, Rick was gone. The man whom my daughter swore she was in love with was dead. I was suddenly a witness to the dark reality of where heroin takes addicts who are not able to successfully battle the demons, and I was even more shaken when I saw the news media accounts of what had happened. Apparently Rick had died during the night after coming home late from a music gig. When those two precious children got up the next morning, they found their father lying on the living room floor.

"Daddy, wake up. Daddy, wake up!" they begged for hours.

By afternoon, those kids did something that was wise beyond their years. They went to the balcony of their apartment and began throwing all kinds of stuff down below. Toys, magazines, small appliances, silverware—whatever they could get their hands on was going over that balcony railing. Sure enough, a neighbor finally caught on to the reality that something was wrong in that apartment and contacted the police. The children had saved themselves and were escorted into the hands of a responsible adult.

One image from the media coverage of this tragedy stuck with me: Misty's knives were among the belongings the children had tossed off the balcony. My daughter was very much a part of this terrible story.

Now, if I am being honest with myself I have to admit that tinged with sadness and remorse over this loss of a young man who could have had a better future was a trace of something else: *relief.* "Cheryl, you're a Christian woman, and this was someone's child who just died,"

I reminded myself. But I couldn't deny that feeling, a relief that this man would no longer be an influence on my daughter. Then I cried, and those thoughts about Misty retreated to a corner of my mind. The thief that is heroin had marched through the door in the dead of night and seized a life. This drug was so hideous!

Soon I wondered about Misty again. Did she know about what had just happened? If not, how should we tell her? How would she react? Would the tragic and sudden loss of her lover totally knock her off her recovery trail? Could Rick still influence her future after all?

When we contacted Roy, he assured us that Misty didn't know about Rick yet. "Please, don't say anything to her," I instructed. "Buddy is going to drive up there to tell her the news."

Even with her father there to comfort her, Misty screamed and cried not only from sadness but a sense of guilt. As best as Buddy could understand from her mostly incoherent explanation, Misty and Rick both had come to the precipice of a fatal heroin overdose before. But each of them relied on the other to kick in certain techniques they had learned from the drug community to pull each other from the ledge. They called it "coming back."

"I should have been there with him," Misty sobbed. "I could have kept Rick alive."

Buddy and the Bridges staff managed to keep Misty there that night, and she was still there when I drove up in daylight hours to complete the gruesome task of bringing her to Rick's apartment. Even though she was still married to Mark and had three beautiful boys of her own, this place had really become Misty's home; she would need to retrieve her belongings. A counselor from Bridges accompanied us to support Misty during this emotional experience. I was ready to stand by my daughter in her grief, but I was not prepared for something else that came up as we rummaged through the sights and smells of drugs and death.

"Mom, look," Misty said casually as she picked up a poster board marked with detailed lines and diagrams. I had been too transfixed by the blood on the walls to notice.

"Yeah, what is that?" I asked.

"It's a schematic I drew of the next hit me and Rick were going to do."

"What did you just say—a *hit*?"

"Yeah, Mom. See, this is the pharmacy we were going to hit next."

"You mean rob it?"

"Yeah, yeah. Look, we've got the exits marked and the place where we were going to enter. We had it all figured out." She sounded proud.

"No, Misty, you aren't serious," I said. "You wouldn't do that."

"Well, we had already done it once. We robbed a gas station at gunpoint."

"You did what? Misty, that's terrible! And how did you manage to do that without being seen or getting caught?"

"Easy, Mom. I dressed up like a guy!"

I had just listened to my daughter admit to and describe being part of an armed robbery and having mapped out a plan to commit another one. And she spoke about it all with an attitude that said, "Look at us!" This was how far down into the gutter heroin and those other drugs had pulled her. This was what my daughter's world looked like with the man she called the "love of my life." I didn't ask Misty any more questions, probably because I was afraid that I would hear about other horrific acts she might have played a part in. Even today, I wonder...and I don't really want to know.

We finished packing up Misty's belongings and stuffed them into the black SUV that was apparently in both hers and Rick's names. She went along with my suggestion to park it outside Mark's house, perhaps as a sign of optimism. Maybe if Misty got cleaned up she would come to realize what she had left behind and want to come back to her "real" home with her husband and three sons. I didn't know how realistic that idea was because I couldn't predict how Misty was going to absorb the reality of her boy-friend's death in the days ahead. All I could do was pray and hope, again, because that's what mothers caught up in this swirling tide of addiction do. Only this time it was more difficult to have faith in a positive outcome.

After appearing to engage in the program briefly, Misty broke the rules again. This time, she and another woman from the program ran off and somehow got hold of some whiskey. When Misty was found drunk and asleep at the park that surrounds the County courthouse in Prescott, she was taken to the ER of the local hospital where she smooth-talked her way out by insisting that her husband was waiting for her outside. The "husband" was actually her female drug dealer. When she eventually found her way back to Bridges, she had crossed a much more severe boundary. She was given an ultimatum: either go into lock-down now or leave. "But I've got to go save those kids," she said in response. She ran off in the middle of the night without telling anyone.

So, as the early autumn easing of the desert heat started to settle in, my daughter began a life on the run. She was running from her loss, running from her husband and children, running from Buddy and me, running from her siblings, running, or trying to run, from her addiction. But that was one spider's nest that wasn't going to let its prey get free.

We heard that she arrested on a DUI while driving the SUV she had picked up from Mark's house. She wound up in jail, but somebody bailed her out before we had a chance to intervene. She still had her 'friends' in the drug underworld, to our frustration and dismay. Every now and then Misty would call us, using someone else's phone. She wouldn't say much, and I was learning not to trust anything she did say anyway. We would try to keep track of her by calling back the last number she had called from, but these people would put me off, making excuses as to why I couldn't speak with her.

"Don't worry, we're keeping Misty clean and sober," they would say. Of course I had no way of knowing if the person making that claim was still even in touch with Misty anymore. One 'friend' must have learned something about me from Misty because he added, "Mrs. Musick, I'm a Christian, too. When Misty came to us, we were committed to helping her get it together. She's doing well, really."

Oh, how I wanted to believe them, and there were moments when I probably did. Other moments I was smart enough to sniff out the lies. It was only later that I gained a more complete picture of Misty's actions and attitude during that time. As it turned out, she wasn't just running away, she was seeking to follow in the footsteps of Rick. And that trail was laced in blood.

Misty's good friend Hailey, who had backed away from Misty during her out-of-control drinking phase, had reached out to her again via email. Misty filled her in about life in the wake of her aborted rehab.

"The first two weeks, I was on a suicide mission," Misty confided. "I was going to try to get enough heroin to follow Rick, and I almost succeeded. I was doing what he was doing his last week, mixing meth into my heroin shots-speed balling. I wanted to feel what he was feeling. It was VERY intense but very scary because you have no idea how strong it is each time. But it's the ultimate rush and high."

Apparently Misty had learned from common friends about how quickly Rick had spiraled down after Misty entered the Bridges program. To hear how she had purposely tried to follow him to the grave gave me chills. That boyfriend was still exerting a major influence on my daughter's health and well-being!

"I'm staying clean now because I know my kids need me," Misty went on to explain to Hailey. "If that is the only reason for staying alive right now, so be it. Hopefully, I will begin to cherish my own life eventually. Right now I feel like the biggest piece of s--- that ever walked the earth. If I would have made a couple of different decisions, would the love of my life still be alive and sober now? We could have had a great life together."

When Hailey tried to reassure her former best friend that she was not to blame for Rick's death, and that she was concerned about how Misty could stay clean without seeking professional help, Misty responded, "I am a stubborn ass girl and even if no one believes me, I have kicked heroin. It took 13 days of hell, and I NEVER want to do that again. I don't care if no one believes me about that. I've just got to live with myself."

To another friend, Sarah, Misty opened up about her whole attraction to Rick, and to the drugs he used to beckon her.

"Rick's wife died of cancer two months before I moved in with him," Misty wrote. "He was banging her pain meds, and when I moved in he asked me if I wanted to try it. Of course I love adventure! I didn't realize that I would fall in love with the drug [heroin]. It is the best, sexiest feeling ever. I hate that I have to know that. We partied a couple times a week, and then it got to be daily. Then it started taking more to feel anything. Heroin is cheaper than Oxycodone ($30 per pill, and we were using anywhere between 20 and 45 pills per day) and at the end, it was taking me 500-600 mg IV Oxycodone plus 3 grams of heroin per day to keep from being sick. Withdrawals if I didn't have enough included shaking, sweating, fever, vomiting, crapping on the bed. I had to keep using to take care of his kids and work. It was a freaking miserable, hopeless way to live. Drugs are freaking amazing, but I literally have lost everything but my clothes. Even the love of my life and two beautiful children who now have no parents. I have a ton of guilt. Wish I could go back in time."

Reading those words from Misty's hand still gives me shivers today. Heroin is "the best, sexiest feeling." Drugs are "freaking amazing." That was the lens my beautiful daughter was looking through during those dark days after her lover's bloody death.

There was more. Misty also told her friend that she was determined to kill herself soon after Rick died and that taking large doses of heroin would be the "best way to die ever." She also shared details about her latest contact, a man who approached her with "a fairly tale offer" that included "Louis Vuitton shoes, a boob job, and a pre-paid apartment for six months." In other words, my darling daughter was being primed for prostitution. At some point she actually told me a more cleaned-up version of this dreamy deal, and I of course did my best to warn her to keep her distance from this sweet-talking dude.

"Mom, no, he's a good guy. He doesn't even use," Misty insisted. Well, pimps don't have to be using drugs to dump more destruction into the lives of those hooked on heroin. And I'm sure he was expecting to make good money off of her. Misty was a very pretty girl.

As those days crept by I sat in dread of receiving that call, the one with the kind of unbearable news that no parent or any loved one should ever hear but almost expects to receive when their child is running with drugs. Buddy and I, Misty's siblings and their spouses or partners, her husband Mark, her three children and so many friends like Hailey who cared so much for Misty were all there waiting for her with open arms. If only she would come to us, we would hold her tight as she tried again to get back on her feet.

Instead, Misty just kept running, now and then slowing down long enough to try to get her loved ones tangled up in the dark mysteries of the trail she had chosen to follow. In late September, she messaged Janelle asking if she could spend the night at her place because the "friend" she was staying with was going out overnight and didn't trust Misty to stay in her home alone. Before Janelle could express her concerns about this arrangement, Misty messaged back: never mind, the friend wasn't going out after all. But the next day Misty contacted Janelle with a new request.

"Sister, there is a shady person looking for me, and I told her I would be with my sister this evening," she wrote. "Please, if you get a message from someone named Angela, just say I'm with you, or if that's uncomfortable, say I'm with Mark. She doesn't know where either of you live."

Janelle was smart and courageous enough to stand firm this time.

"How would I get a call?" she wrote. "I hope my number is not given out. I don't want to be involved with any shady people."

Fortunately, Janelle did not receive any calls or messages about Misty then, and the next day Misty explained more about her living situation.

"Keep this info to yourself because you know how Mom feels about people who have contributed to my addiction, but Angela is my old oxy dealer and she got us the heroin the first couple times we did it. She is helping me out right now, but she still deals and there are some days I struggle and just need to get away. People are over every day throughout the day smoking meth. But it's actually one of the safer places I have been. I'm learning some tough life lessons right now. I have been doing really well, actually. She is like a mom to me, but there are tough days, and I have to get away."

Living with her former drug dealer was going to help her get her life straight? That's how far Misty had plunged since leaving her recovery program. Her thinking had become even more twisted and distorted.

My contact with Misty had slowed to a trickle. From the little bits of information I would pick up, my head was filled with all sorts of frightful images of her running the streets, hanging out with people who claimed to be protecting her but in reality were probably using her for drugs or sex while plotting bolder and more destructive actions that could destroy her. How and where was this all going to end?

One night, soon after Misty's attempt to get Janelle caught in her spider's web, Misty actually texted me.

"Mom, I need to talk to you."

"What's going on?" I immediately texted back, trying not to let my imagination fill in the blanks.

"Just call me right now!" she texted back.

I took a breath and grabbed my cell. I barely had time to say hello and ask if she was alright when she blurted out what had driven her to contact me.

"Mom, was Rick planning to cheat on me? Was he already cheating on me before I went to rehab?" Misty asked.

She knew that I had been in contact with Rick's step-mother-in-law and probably others who knew Rick and the whole crazy relationship.

"Sweetie, I don't know for sure," I said. "But from what I was told, your boyfriend was pretty skanky. He probably was seeing other women when he was with you."

"Yeah, I thought he was," she snarled. "I thought I loved him but he was screwing around and he was lying to me. I thought I could trust him!"

She went on and on about this, and after awhile it all sounded like gibberish. Was she high? Maybe. Or maybe she was actually clean and this was a desperate attempt to wake up to the truth about the man she had been living with. With Misty, it was always hard to know. She did make it clear she was not interested in filling me in on anything else about her current situation. There were so many questions that I desperately wanted to ask: Was she safe? Was she sober? Was she eating? How was she finding the money to support herself? Where was she actually living? What was she going to do and where was she going to go next? Was she even considering going back to treatment?

That brief phone call ended with no answers, which sure wasn't going to help me get any sleep that night. The next day, I decided I had to at least try to find out something about Misty's living situation. She didn't answer when I called, of course. So I texted her: "Misty where are you? What's going on?" No text reply.

I did not know it then but during those long hours while I waited for any kind of text message back from my daughter, she was busy texting someone else. The cryptic words she shared in those texts would wind up steering Misty down a new and darker hallway. All I knew that night and early the next morning was that I had reached my limit of waiting and worrying. I had to know *something*, whatever it was, about my daughter's welfare. And my maternal instinct was leading me in the direction of where to take my questions next. I called the police in Prescott Valley, where I assumed she was still living.

"My daughter is running the streets and I'm terrified about what is happening to her," I explained. "Do you have any information about Misty Musick Sanchez?"

After a long pause, the officer came back on the line.

"Your daughter has been arrested," he said calmly.

Was it the tone of his voice, or a mother's instinct, or perhaps a message from God that steered me to the immediate conclusion that this was not just another DUI, some offense that could be dealt with in the matter of hours or a few days, with Misty allowed to continue on her wild, destructive path? This was serious, *very* serious.

"What has happened to my daughter?" I wailed. "What did she do?"

She was being held in jail in Prescott. I don't pretend to know the full story of the shocking incident that unfolded during the night while I was trying so frantically to reach Misty to find out if she was okay. Even after hearing Misty's version and reading the police reports, it all just seemed like one hideous, terrifying mess that probably was never going to be completely and honestly sorted out. Did the details really matter? This was the picture the best I could make of it:

Misty had been staying with Angela, who had informed Misty she would need to find a new place to live soon. Angela still had many of Misty's belongings in her home, most likely because Misty had given them to her in return for drugs. Misty wanted her stuff back before she took off...for somewhere. So she conspired with some guy to stage a break-in during which he would seize Misty's stuff, and probably more than that. Misty even tipped him off to a trick she had learned while living there: how to get into the house via a pet entry and avoid surveillance cameras that could pick up incriminating evidence. That night Misty conveniently unlocked the door for him.

Misty's co-conspirator apparently had his own ideas about how this plan was going down. Dressed all in black, his face covered in a ski mask, he burst through the door and immediately tied up Misty's hands and loosely gagged her, perhaps to give her a "cover story" that she was not involved with what happened next. Because what did happen after Misty was bound is almost too brutal for me to report.

The masked man charged into Angela's bedroom and held a knife to her throat. "Open the damn safe!" he screamed. Misty had told him about Angela's safe, which Misty had reason to believe contained a large sum of money. When Angela tried to fight him off, he beat her severely: fractured ribs, cracked vertebrae, bruised lung, blackened eyes, torn off lip, multiple stitches in her face. That trail of blood that Misty had been following since Rick OD'd had taken a new and sickening turn.

Misty was "held" in the bathroom with Angela while the thief rummaged through the house. He never did get into the safe, leaving with computer equipment, a TV and a few other things he could round up. Angela was treated at a hospital and the police were brought in.

At first, Misty stuck to her story that she was just an innocent bystander, but the evidence on her phone told a very different story. She was in communication with the thief about what to do in the hours and minutes leading up to his arrival. After Misty snuck into Angela's house first, she texted her co-conspirator: "You're good to go." She also confirmed to him that Angela was asleep. There was no question that Misty was complicit in the crime and would have to pay for her actions.

At least she demonstrated some integrity. When police initially arrested a man whom Angela identified as her attacker, Misty stepped forward to declare that it was not him who conspired with her to enter Angela's home. She provided information leading to the arrest of the guy who actually did it. The charges against Misty sounded ominous:

- Conspiracy to commit burglary in the first degree
- Armed robbery
- Burglary in the first degree
- Kidnapping
- Two counts of aggravated assault

Oh, but that was not the full extent of the criminal problems hovering over my daughter's head. In addition to that serious list of offenses related to the theft and assault at Angela's house, Misty also faced charges connected with that incident in August when she drove Rick's van into a ditch while high on drugs: possession of a narcotic drug and drug paraphernalia; two DUI counts; theft and illegal possession of prescription medication. That last reference to prescription drugs came from Misty and Rick getting caught on security cameras illegally obtaining medication that was supposed to go to Misty's hospice patients. Misty had been stealing from those in her care, leaving them to suffer additional pain and suffering. That is how low my precious daughter had stooped while in the clutches of addiction.

I was mostly numb during those first days after Misty was secured behind bars. I was horrified but not shocked. Misty had shown me those poster boards mapping out an armed robbery she and Rick had planned and bragged about committing one before that. She was certainly capable of serious criminal behavior. I did believe her when she insisted that she had no idea that Angela was going to be beaten and would never physically harm anyone herself.

Most of my attention was focused on the practical questions: what was going to happen to Misty now? How could Buddy and I help her? I gasped when I heard talk that her charges could result in a sentence of up to 100 years, but insiders reassured me that police and prosecutors routinely use scare tactics during investigations before matters could be resolved in court.

I did my best to summon that attitude I had recently attempted to live by: the addict is separate from the person. The Misty that I had known and raised would never be a part of anything like this. The addict, however, had become fully capable of what had happened, and more. Misty was held tightly within the grasp of the addict and was powerless to act any differently.

Another thought swooped in: *So this is what rock bottom looks like.* As addicts everywhere and those who assist them in recovery know well, rock bottom is that place where drugs have driven you to your absolute lowest point. It's usually some kind of physical, mental, emotional or criminal crisis. The good news is that rock bottom *can* become the starting point for getting well. When circumstances prevent you from continuing your destructive behavior, you have a choice of what to do from there.

Well, Misty was going to be in a secured environment, away from all drugs (if rules in jail are followed!), and left to face herself and all her demons for quite a long time. She would be provided ample opportunities to make choices about where she was going from here.

Coming face-to-face with the reality of my daughter living behind bars, entering a long and impactful period of reflection and resolution, I could be sure of only one thing. As her mother, I would stand by her every step of the way, providing all the love, compassion, encouragement, understanding, guidance, patience, faith and prayer that I could possibly muster.

"Dear God," I prayed, "show me the strength to do what I need to do."

CHAPTER 6

— ✂ —

Letters from the Yavapai County Jail

As MOST LOVED ones of women and men who have spent prolonged periods in jail know very well, trying to maintain any meaningful contact with someone behind bars can make you crazy. You just can't communicate the way you are used to and want so desperately to do during this trying time.

When you visit the inmate in person, you are stripped of all privacy. Sitting in a stone walled waiting room wearing a numbered badge and listening to other inmate family conversations is maddening enough, but by the time you are finally called, walk through the security body scanner and arrive at your numbered booth, you realize you have to speak into a phone receiver and see your loved one through a thick plate of glass. You can't even hug! Phone calls from home are costly and limited, with the constant anxiety over when that mechanical voice that will come over the line to tell you your time is almost up. You can forget about emails and text messages, at least in my experience with Misty in 2013-14. With all the rules and regulations, you feel like your hands are tied.

Well, I didn't like all those roadblocks when my daughter settled into her life wearing the orange outfit of an inmate in October 2013, but I was determined that they would not stop me from fulfilling my mission to be there for her. I simply turned back the hands of time and communicated the way our grandparents did: snail mail. I wrote dozens and dozens of letters to Misty, and I was heartened to find that she was willing to write back. Another frustrating rule restricted how often she could write, but those letters she did write from the Yavapai County jail were of tremendous comfort to me during those long weeks and months of not knowing what was going to happen to her.

Excerpts from our mother-daughter letter-writing campaign capture glimpses into my swirling emotions—all the sadness, fear, desperation and grief, mixed with waves of confidence, joy, faith and hope.

10/16/13

Misty,

I finally figured out how to communicate with you. Trying to understand all the rules and regulations here has been so difficult. Dad is trying so hard to get your phone account set up but at least we know what happened to the money he deposited. It's actually sitting in another Arizona jail account. Not sure how that happened. The system is crazy. He is trying to get it transferred to you with great difficulty.

We are heading up to PV (Prescott Valley) Sunday for Carlos' B-day party. We all pitched in to help Mark buy some really nice skates for him and he is excited. We will spend the night so we can be with you in court.

No matter what, Misty, we love you and are praying for you.

See you soon – Mom

A few days later I wrote Misty again, filling her in on the birthday party and other family news. Shannon and Brent had selected the name of Emmett for their baby boy on the way, and Janelle and I made plans for the baby shower. Buddy and I bought Josh's cap and gown for his graduation the following June. Josh went skateboarding with Misty's boys during the birthday festivities. I made sure to end on a more personal and hopeful note about Misty: "No matter how bleak your situation seems, I choose to see the light at the end of the tunnel. I know that God has a plan and I am determined to 'Praise Him in the Storm.'

Praying that he will bring you strength and comfort in your heart and soul."

The first letter from Misty was dated October 22, 2013:

Dear Mom, Dad, Grandma & Josh,

Well here I am. What a s---t show. I get what's called a "poor boy," which is paper and an envelope once a week since I still have no money on my books. Guys, I can't stress to you how bad I need money in here. It is automatically $60 per month, so I'm in the hole already for this stay and the last time as well. I need shampoo, soap and some food. I am starving in here. Phone calls and envelopes would be nice too. Phone calls are $6 per call in the local area. Very frustrating.

I've been doing yoga and kickboxing in the mornings. I'm sore! Trying to build back some muscle mass. I'm back up to 147 pounds, and I would like to stay at that weight. I'm enclosing notes for the boys. Please deliver them.

All I know is I'm stuck in here until 11/25 when I have my next court date. Who knows what will happen that day? I'll try to keep you posted after speaking with my lawyer. Josh, I love you very much. Grandma, they refused your letter to me—Mom, explain the rules to her? The more letters the better. Mom, please print out a pic of me and Rick and send it, as well as a more recent pic of all 5 kids please. Thank you. Please also get on Facebook and send my mailing address to my girlfriend Sarah.

Love always,

Misty

P.S. Dad, my truck was dumped. Don't make payments. It's a loss. I can't trust anyone. F---ing a---hole.

Many of Misty's early letters from jail sounded demanding, whining or self-absorbed. Her words sometimes stung, but I tried to keep in mind the trauma she had just experienced in hitting rock bottom and being a witness to the severe beating of her former "roommate" and ex-drug dealer. Then again, in one way or another we all shared the trauma of what was happening and the fear of what was to come.

10/26/13

Dear Misty,

You are being blamed for some big things, and frankly we don't think you're safe in Prescott and Prescott Valley. Mark is concerned for the safety of the boys, too. The drug world is full of deception, hate and danger. All I can do is pray that you, your boys, and we will all be safe.

We will do the best we can to keep money in your commissary account. There may be a few people who can help and others who won't because of why you are in jail in the first place. We all want you to go to Rehab. We all want you to address your drug and alcohol addictions which have had a major affect on our entire family. I'm not trying to cause more pain but hoping you will see that there is much more pain ahead for us all if you do not go through the recovery process. Not trying to be a therapist but a very concerned Mother and grandmother. Dad agrees as well as your siblings.

I love you Daughter and will keep the letters coming. Be strong, be wise. Praying for you daily.

Love, Mom

As the mother of six children, I thought it was important for Misty to see the pain that her actions had caused us and continued to bring to us. I also wanted her to know that we were all rooting for her to open up to the recovery process, for her own health first and foremost and for our well-being as a family too. Misty didn't want to hear any of this.

10/27/13

Dear Family,

I know you guys think the worst of me, but I really was doing better before I came back here again. Don't believe everything you hear, please. Please thank Pastor Duane and Shannon for writing letters on my behalf. I need Shannon to be less angry and judgmental. I hope she never has to walk for a minute in my shoes. This has been the hardest year of my life, and I have thought several times of ending it. Please give me some grace.

At night I lay on a thin mat with a Mexican type blanket on the floor. I'm still in a lot of pain from my accident in August. I'm worried that I have a fractured thoracic vertebrae or a bulging disk. I feel like even my siblings have abandoned me when I need them the most. I know I've screwed up, but isn't love supposed to be unconditional? No letters in 3 weeks? Not one of them can spare $10? After everything I've done for them in the past—vehicles given, a roof and meals, education and support. I'm pretty hurt. If any one of them were in my boat, I would bend over backwards to help. Like I said, I hope none of you ever have to know what my life feels like, but if you did the response might be different. I also know you all think rehab is the answer. I disagree. I felt worse there than I do here. I want to get on probation with drug testing and get back to work and school.

Anyway, I have some really bad days in here when I just want to follow Rick. Other days I'm full of hope and joy. I make people laugh and have several girls working out with me. There are some amazing women in here and some not so amazing women as well. I've been participating in daily Bible studies and I lead them in a cappella worship. Again, can't stress how much commissary money is needed. My hair is greasy and I'm _hungry!_ Please! Mom, feel free to share my letters since I only get to write 1 per week. Tell Carlos, B (Brendon) and Josiah that I adore them and to be brave. Pray for God's favor in my life and cases.

Love you all!

Misty

I was hurt by Misty's defensiveness and accusations toward our family. I knew that I had to stick up for my children, but I also didn't want to drive Misty further away. If she decided to stop communicating with me, I was afraid I would never be able to help her get well. Trying to maintain that delicate balance was keeping me up at night.

10/30/13

Dearest Daughter,

I want to thank you for sharing your heart-felt thoughts in your last letter. Please try to understand the toll this has taken on our family and the roller coaster ride your addictions have caused us all. Your alcohol addiction was frightening enough, but what came next was closer to terror. We all had such hope when you were in treatment, but you broke rules while there. Rehab is supposed to be hard—it doesn't feel good facing your demons. It scares me because I know you have so much pain and unresolved issues inside, but you keep running from them.

We are all terrified that you will get out and go back to using, which is a very real possibility without professional help/support. Michael is frightened for you, Brian is stressed, Janelle is concerned for her safety, Shannon's frustrated, Josh is hurt and angry. They would not be having these feelings if they didn't love you. You told me that you were having fun those days with Rick. We were scared for your life while you were partying. We want you to find yourself—the real, precious Misty, not the person you think we want you to be, not the alcoholic or heroin addict

Misty but the Misty you were created to be. Your siblings will have to work out their individual feelings. I know they love you. Dad and I are here for you, but only for you—your addictions are not welcome. We hate them because they want to destroy our beautiful daughter, her sons and her entire family.

 We will continue to pray, love you and send what we can to help. I love you so much.

 Mom

10/31/13

Dear Mom & Dad,

 Mom, thanks for your honesty in your last letter, but I again have to say that I refuse to be "punished" by family for my choices. They either love me or they don't. I need to do what's best for me and my kids. None of you know what that looks like. I will not be told by family that rehab is a condition for love and acceptance. If I have to go by order of the court, I will do so, but not until then. I will never forget how I'm being treated, and that sucks. My relationship with the people I love will never be the same. I'm done giving and caring what others think. Again, I hope none of them ever have to experience half of what I have.

I understand that the defiance and manipulation, and the unwilling-ness to take any responsibility for her actions, was Misty's addiction talking. As painful as it was to read her words, I just kept reminding myself that the Misty underneath her addictions would not think, talk or act that way toward those who loved her. I clung to the faith that her behavior and her relationships could change over time.

 Anyway, not all her relationships were on rocky ground. In those early days in jail, Buddy was able to have a long, private talk with Misty in which they cleared the air about their past relationship and opened the door to a much more positive father-daughter connection.

11/5/13

Dearest Misty,

Dad told me about your conversation with tears in his eyes. I feel strongly that you both needed that father/daughter time. He told me he feels badly that he wasn't the greatest father for you when you were growing up. I reminded him that he was a great provider and that's all he knew to do—work and provide_and he said, "Well that's more than my Dad did."

I can't help but believe that God is using these "misadventures" to bring healing. Your Dad got teary eyed several times while talking about you. You are loved so much_and believe it or not you are loved by your siblings. Though they have no clue (thankfully) what's in like to be in your shoes (orange flops) we have no idea what it is like to be in theirs—shock, dismay, confusion, pain, fear. Most of them do not fully understand what drug addiction does to people, and causes them to do, since our family has never been exposed to hard drugs. I'm not trying to make excuses for them, but simply hoping you'll not get hurt and you'll give them some time. Our entire family is grappling with what has gone on and what is to come.

Thankfully, Misty eased up on her accusations. "I know my siblings love me. It's OK. I just needed to express my feelings," she wrote, and she expressed remorse over her behavior to at least one person, her husband Mark: "Why is he such a great man? I've done nothing but hurt him again and again, yet he still has my back. Ugh…I hate myself." She shared a hopeful future image of having a campfire with her family and roasting s'mores dipped in peanut butter. She also expressed gratitude for my efforts in supporting her: "Thank you for your letters. They mean the world to me. Please, though, no more talk about rehab. It's irrelevant at this point. I love you, Mom. Thanks for loving me no matter what."

You can bet that message went right through to this mother's heart! When Misty made a reference to rehab being "irrelevant" she didn't just mean that she was opposed to drug treatment. She also meant that since she was in jail, she would not have access to alcohol and drugs for a long, indefinite period.

Still, we all wanted so badly for Misty to seek drug treatment. While prosecutors assessed Misty's many charges and her lawyers argued for lesser penalties, we all believed that Misty's sentence absolutely had to include some mandatory drug and alcohol rehab. I wrote impassioned letters to her judge to argue for this, and so did many other members of our family. All our pleas were ignored. Throughout this entire ordeal, drug rehab was never linked to my daughter's penalties for the drug-triggered crimes that she committed. There were no directives to complete any kind for residential drug treatment program, no requirement to regularly attend NA or AA meetings, no mandate to see a therapist specializing in drug and alcohol recovery—nothing but fines to pay, community service hours to fill, visits to her PO and attendance to some sort of life skills class. To me, this was a horrible and incomprehensible failure on the part of our criminal justice system, and I did not and have not forgotten that!

Like it or not, Misty's "treatment" was to sit for hour upon hour every day in her jail cell trying to figure out how to rebuild her life on her own. And she was making strides. It was encouraging to hear that she was practicing yoga and even teaching yoga classes. I could imagine her helping some of the older inmates, women whose creaking bodies were bound with stiffness to get off their bunks and get moving. She was also leading Bible study classes and singing groups. I began sending her inspirational Bible passages and lyrics from songs that I thought she would enjoy, trying to feed her anything that could encourage her recovery. First and foremost, that meant keeping up with my letter-writing.

11/12/13

Dear Misty,

I miss you, Sweetie! I'm sitting at my usual spot at the table with my Bible sipping coffee, just wishing this were only a terrible dream and we could wake up and there you would be in your soft fluffy robe sipping coffee with me. I have hope for you, my Daughter, though this isn't nearly what I envisioned for your life. But the twists, turns and even the crevices in the road can still lead to hope, victory and peace. I pray for peace—my prayers are what hold me together. I need them or I'll not be able to function. I pray for you to have peace in the midst of this terrible storm.

In another letter I admitted to Misty that I sometimes wondered what Buddy and I had done wrong that could have contributed to her choice to abuse alcohol and drugs. "I know we made mistakes—Dad was the military father and I was the hovering helicopter mother—but I've been told by my therapist and friends to avoid placing blame. I try," I wrote.

Misty didn't bring up any mistakes that I made while she was growing up, but she did express anger for something that had happened more recently. She had given me her Facebook password with specific directions about what she wanted me to do with her account. I admit that I went further—I read some of the messages that she had shared with her Facebook friends.

"I'm hurt, Mom," Misty wrote. "I feel violated, like there is nothing left that is only mine. You don't get to know every innermost detail." In complaining about this to others in our family, Misty also brought up how angry she had been several months earlier when she had finally admitted to me that she was using heroin and I immediately informed all her siblings. Here's how I responded to that: "When I confronted you (about using heroin) I was treated and spoken to as a child—reprimanded. I told you that you could die and you laughed at me. This was absolute agony. I knew there was a chance you would borrow money to support your expensive habit so I broke the silence to your siblings."

As for Misty's accusation that I was treating her like an adolescent for "snooping" on her Facebook account, I was furious. Yes, I did "snoop," and I'll never apologize for that. I believed that our lives were at risk because of the seedy, dangerous people she had been in contact with, and I needed information that would help me protect my family. I was still the lioness!

"What I did was not treating you like an adolescent," I explained. "I don't need any more adolescents and frankly, people on drugs ACT like rebellious adolescents with their stealing, rash decisions, irresponsible behavior and placing others in dangerous situations."

I was also angry, and hurt, after coming across a Facebook message that Rick had sent to Misty while she was in treatment at Bridges, right after he and I had that heated talk about his "Father of the Year" credentials. Rick told Misty that he hated me so much that he wanted to chop off my head…and shove it up my a-- !

The amazing thing about this latest mother-daughter tussle was that it didn't last. Misty and I both said what we needed to say, and then went right back to writing in a kinder and more respectful tone. I give credit to my daughter for her willingness to focus on the present and the love that we really did share.

Our family missed Misty that Thanksgiving, and when I wrote to her soon after the holiday I tried to comfort her by telling her that "I know God has plans for your life." I shared a psalm that spoke to my wishes:

"For I know the plans I have for you, declares the Lord, plans to prosper you and not harm you, plans to give you hope and a future." – Jeremiah 29:11.

While we made plans for Christmas at home without Misty, she focused on her work: keeping herself fit and continuing to serve as a leader among inmates with her worship meetings, singing and yoga classes. She also devoted time to consoling first-time detainees who came in confused and frightened. And instead of defending her behavior, she began to open up to her real feelings underneath the anger and defiance.

12/14/13

Dear Mom,

Thank you for your consistent letters. I look forward to them so much! I have been struggling this week. The sense of loss I am experiencing is incredibly deep. I can't dream or plan my future because I don't know what I'm facing. I feel so alone. I want to hold my children. The pain and loss I've caused is overwhelming.

I tried to cheer Misty up with silly drawings, and she sent me drawings of her own along with a witty poem about jail life. That was the Misty I had known. I felt so sad that she missed Christmas and even sadder when she wrote, "I hope you guys had a great Christmas. I tried to sleep and read most of the day so it would pass quickly." As I read those words, I spoke a silent wish that her next Christmas would somehow be a brighter and more uplifting day—like Christmas is meant to be!

On New Year's Eve, I wrote that my wish for Misty for the year ahead was "to desire, above all else, God's will for your life, to allow Him to take over, for complete surrender, to be still, rest, to quietly listen for His still small voice to lead you; to have peace, no matter the circumstances."

I kept Misty abreast of all the latest family birthdays and gatherings. During a visit with Mark and Misty's three boys, Mark told me that Misty used to feel judged by me after she and her family would visit us during the holidays. I knew that what she was saying was true, and that my judgments were not limited to my reaction when she tried to use my blender to make margaritas that one time. "I have been a judgmental person in the past and I have been working so hard to love people right where they're at," I wrote. I realized that this change in me was actually one gift born out of all this suffering over my daughter's addiction. Maybe we were both becoming more honest with ourselves, and with each other.

In mid-January, as her lawyers continued to negotiate a possible plea and reasonable jail sentence with probation, Misty reflected on how she had reached this point:

1/17/14

Mom,

I can't sleep at night I just keep picturing my sons in my arms. The State Board of Nursing allowed me to make changes to my license surrender document. My nursing license is revoked officially as of 1/16/13. I have a hole in my heart the size of Texas, and my throat has a lump in it every time I think of that I'm so ashamed. Reading the 'Findings of Fact' section in the court records made me want to hide in a hole. They talked to Bridges, the rehab hospital I worked at, the hospice program I worked for, and they have all my police reports. It's an ugly picture of me. I wrote the Attorney General a letter describing my past year and expressing remorse.

Sorry my letter is so bleak. That's just where I've been for a couple of weeks. Your letters mean so much to me. Sometimes it's just hard to write back. Please keep praying for a merciful plea. I miss my family so much it hurts.

I did keep praying for Misty, and in the middle of that winter I also needed to focus more prayers on my husband. Buddy and I spent several days in Minnesota where he sought explanations and treatment for his troubling health issues. He didn't get all the answers he was hoping for, unfortunately, but the time away provided a break from the intensity of our daughter's life in jail and allowed me to visit with Valerie, one of my oldest and dearest friends I've known since attending Faye Ross Jr. High School in Artesia.

Back home, I scrambled to catch up with work and get back in the flow of family life. Shannon's twenty-first birthday and birth of her son Emmett were approaching, and I got to take Carlos, Brendon and Josiah to the Jump Street trampoline park in Glendale and to a skate park. But when it was time for Misty to appear in court, Buddy and I were right there in Prescott to witness it.

Those are images I wish I didn't have to revisit: Misty in her orange jail scrubs, shackled with chains and handcuffed, shuffling into the courthouse with a group of inmates being escorted by corrections officers into the elevator and ordered to face the rear wall inside; Misty walking from the court to the hallway where I so desperately wanted to reach out and touch her through the glass partition that kept us apart. At least I could see her face without glass inside the courtroom, where she managed to exchange goofy grins with us at the sight of one of the lawyers that Buddy called Pee Wee Herman.

For Valentine's Day, I sent Misty a drawing of the green candy dish that she always knew she would find on my table when she visited us. If she couldn't actually reach her hands inside and scoop out her favorite candy, she could at least imagine it. I labeled the pieces of candy hearts in my drawing with the traits that I saw in my daughter: amazing, witty, beautiful, precious, talented, intelligent, caring, and loving.

When I wrote to Misty with the details of Emmett's birth, she said, "I bawled like a baby when I read your letter. I wish I could have seen Brent's face! I am missing so much." As she continued to wait for a court resolution, she wrestled with her emotions:

"The hardest pain of all this waiting is my own brain. It never stops. I relive the last year over and over. Then I think of all the things I want in my life. The only time my mind is quiet is when I do yoga. Then I can pray and feel relief, if only for an hour. The message I hear when I practice lately is 'Let your heart's intentions become your conscious mind.' My heart is almost always in the right place, but my messed up head gets in the way. I manipulate myself into thinking my crazy ideas are good ideas."

Some of her crazier ideas came out when she obsessed about the details of Rick's death. She kept asking questions, wondering what really happened. There were no concrete answers to be found and, as I wrote her, "This entire story is worse than a soap opera—and sadly it's real." It took a long time for Misty to let go of asking "why" and when she was able to do that, she became even more of a leader among her fellow inmates. "Many girls look up to me. I do my best to live in the moment and bring light to those around me," she noted. When the other inmates pointed out that Misty received more letters from home than all the rest of them, she was able to acknowledge that she felt blessed for her family's support.

Our letters continued to build on the closeness between us, and during one visit in jail it all began to sink in. Misty was changing. The addict had been shoved aside and the person that was Misty was beginning to shine through. Our talk together in jail was just real, like the loving mother and daughter I knew we could be. I broke down in tears at how far we had come together.

3/5/14

Dear Misty,

Oh My Goat! I enjoyed our visit so much. The honesty and openness was so valuable and precious. I miss you. I miss your hugs and our moments over coffee. I will value our conversation and shared tears for the rest of my life. My tears were not sad—I saw you mouthing the words 'It's okay,' but I was just so full of love for you and grateful that you are beginning the healing process. You are climbing out of the box—the box that has held you captive to the expectations of others. Life is not a performance and you can now gracefully step off the stage, find yourself and embrace the woman you are meant to be.

At the end of that letter I drew a horse. Would she remember the ride we shared on the Verde River before heroin had clutched her by the throat? It seemed as if it would never let go, but now here she was, clean and sober and getting physically, emotionally and spiritually stronger.

In March, attorneys on her case worked out a tentative plea agreement. Misty would remain in jail for about one more year, although she was pursuing a position as an inmate worker that could push the clock ahead. Not everything was in place yet, but at least we had some answers. None of us liked the idea of Misty being incarcerated for many more months but I also recognized that jail, strangely enough, was turning out to be a good place for her at this time in her life. "To know that you have found calm and peace in a county jail is amazing," I wrote. And I firmly believed that with faith, we could all ride out the duration of time away and then welcome the "real Misty" back in our day-to-day lives.

It was during this time that Misty surprised me with a new idea of what she would do after her release.

"I wonder if you, Mark & Shannon can save the letters I have been sending to you from here," she wrote. "They will assist me in a blog I want to start when I get out. Maybe my journey will help someone someday. I'm thinking the title will be 'To the Brink.' Just an idea. Your thoughts, Mom?"

My response: "I love your idea of a blog! I've actually considered doing the same thing from my perspective to help families of other inmates and addicts."

That's when the idea of publicly sharing our thoughts, feelings and experiences during Misty's journey with addiction began to take root. I vowed to do my best to keep nurturing its growth. If God had a plan for my daughter and me to reach out to others through writing, I would open my arms wide to it. I had come to realize that what happened to Misty, and to all of us who loved her, can happen to anyone, even those who may seem to be the best of people and the nicest of families. And when the hurricane stormed through their lives, I would want them to feel as if they were not alone.

On April 16, I honored my daughter on her thirty-third birthday with cards that several of us drew for her and a note: "I was just remembering that beautiful Christmas dinner you made for the Sanchez/Musick families. Such love you placed into each morsel, every place card personalized with love. THAT is the Misty I know, and the good caring heart that I remember...Wish I could hug you today but these hugs are being stored up for the day I <u>can</u> hug you—and you will be well hugged!"

In her response, Misty asked, "Do you have a friend who might let me ride one of their horses? I would like to go on a ride with you when I am out of here." This mother's heart melted even more. My beautiful daughter remembered that ride along the river we shared together before her life plunged further into the darkness of addiction and she wanted to enjoy that experience with me again.

Of course, Misty and I still hit our little blips in the road together. Our mother-daughter relationship would almost seem incomplete if we didn't! When her plea agreement was finalized in court, and Misty read all the letters of support that her family had written to the judge on her behalf, she rebelled against some of the characterizations of her addictive tendencies and personality.

"This is who I am...I have a zest for life!" she proclaimed to the whole family. "I like to learn things and use my body and push the limits. I do have a problem with substance abuse and will deal with it—on <u>my own terms</u>! But I'm never going to stop being the person I am and you better not ask me to. The day that you convince me to stop is the day my life is no longer worth living."

She took a few more shots, including another one aimed at me for my judgmental ways toward her. I took my time in carefully responding to her with empathy, openness about my own experience and a little humor. Since my letter was dated May 8, I signed off "Happy Friggin' Mother's Day to Us!" And everything between us was fine again.

Misty also wrote to the judge, admitting to her mistakes and making a plea for that inmate worker position. She admitted that "coming to jail has saved my life." While she awaited word on that front, she wrote to me about the life she imagined when she finally did get out.

"I dream of hiking with Carlos, taking B out shopping and snuggling with Josiah with hot cocoa. I want to take my sons out on dates and enjoy the rest of their childhoods. And I can't wait to play music with them. Those are the things I'm most looking forward to."

My daughter had sure come a long way from the woman who proclaimed to friends that she was tired of being a mother while locking herself away at her boyfriend's home. It was one more healthy change that I rejoiced at witnessing. Of course, it was very painful for Carlos, Brendon and Josiah to visit their mother in jail, separated by glass and able to speak with her only on the phone. Mark told me they would cry on the way home after every visit. Like me, Misty's sons also turned to letter-writing to keep their connection with their mom alive.

In June, I took another step forward with the idea of Misty and me teaming up to help other people by telling our stories. "Perhaps you and I can co-author a book and share our mother-daughter perspectives on this journey," I wrote. "I think that would be cool, but it would be your call for sure. I think it may help others who find themselves in similar circumstances."

Misty responded right away: "When you mentioned writing a book, that's one of the reasons I'm asking people to save my letters. They will remind me of what I was feeling each month I have been in here. I thought of a blog first, though. Blogs are accessible and easy to start. Lots of books start out this way. I want it to be very raw and honest. I know other people will gain insight or encouragement from it."

Building on the idea of helping others, I added: "I know that this journey has changed us all, and for myself for the better. Less judgmental, more insight, ministry ideas—more love for the wounded, more street-wise. On and on..."

Misty maintained her role as an inmate leader. After hearing that many of the other women lacked a high school diploma or a GED, she hunkered down to teach them basic math and algebra every day. When their hard work was done, she would gather them together in a more spiritual environment. As she described it:

"Our dorm joins hands in a giant circle around the Day Room every night before lockdown for nightly prayer. This week, there are about 40 girls coming together. It's a big circle! I'm very happy and content and have been feeling that way pretty consistently."

With this glorious picture of Misty bringing women together in jail, I wrote back: "My heart swells with pride and wants to burst with happiness. You are ministering—it doesn't have to happen on a church platform. How wonderful!"

By the start of summer, we were already discussing plans for Misty to stay in our home for awhile after she was released so that she would have time to get back on her feet and sort out her next steps in life. With this idea in mind, I wrote: "The thought of you snuggled in the bed of our guest room is so comforting, Misty. There was a time that I wondered if I'd ever see you again. My first born—my beautiful, precious Daughter!"

Misty dug even deeper into her personal growth, reading books about prayer, meditation and living in the present moment. Here's how she explained some of these new teachings:

"It's very basic and honest truths, nothing far out or weird. And it's all about getting rid of the crap in our lives so we can live deeper and more fully in the arms of God. When I practice yoga, my mind becomes quiet enough so I can sometimes feel God's hand reach into my chest and cover the wounds of my heart with his big, warm hand. It feels like a huge hug, and I can feel his perfect love and grace. What a gift—to feel that in jail, and share it with others!"

She balanced these spiritual visions with pragmatic wishes for her first meal back home: my homemade coffee cake, rib-eye steak, a beautiful salad with balsamic oil and vinegar and cracked pepper, a sweet potato with butter, a honey crisp apple and Ben & Jerry's ice cream. She also yearned to "Roast marshmallows with her sons and fall asleep in a dog pile with them. I want to run and feel the breeze in my face. I want to feel the grass under my feet!"

Joining in the spirit of Misty's images of a positive future, I wrote:

"Please, let's dance when you get here—dance like nobody is watching! I can't get Dad to dance with me, but I know you will! And I can't wait to hug you, to see your face up close, to listen to you sing, to see your silliness, to sip coffee with you, to sit on the porch swing with you, to witness your eyes and the eyes of your sons when you first greet each other, to touch your hair. To smell its scent when I hug you—to be able to touch you—it's been so hard having you so close when we visit and not being able to touch you! To see you in pajamas, to watch the sunrise together, to see you hug your Daddy."

Now I have to be honest here about something. Not every day in my life was filled with idyllic images of Misty's return. At times my enthusiasm was pushed aside by the sadness I still felt over how far she had fallen and my anxiety about how she was going to stay clean and sober without structured support, ON HER TERMS! Would she be able to fight off the demons if they came knocking on her door when she was out in the world free again? I wanted to believe she could, but I knew enough about recovery to understand that without help, it was going to be a monumental challenge. With that fear hovering over my shoulder, I sometimes struggled to get out of bed in the morning and I was gaining weight from turning to comfort food.

I also had to face the grief from the loss of two special animals: Emma, one of the miniature horses I cared for and worked with at Rosewood Ranch, and Cash, my 5 yr. old Black Lab therapy dog partner. Cash lived with me and his death was sudden and unexpected; internal bleeding from a softball sized tumor on his pancreas. This sad event was to be kept quiet through the weekend until our entire clinical team could be on hand to support the patients. By Monday morning my sense of loss and stress triggered vomiting and diarrhea. It was a painful blow for me, and I worried about how my patients would handle the news. They were very attached to both of these wonderful animals. This happened in July which I thought strange as my Dad had died in July, later Mom's second Husband Larry died of a stroke in July, and now these two precious therapy animals.

Thankfully, the calendar turned a page, and by August Misty was working in the jail's laundry room, living in nicer and more private quarters and marking off the days until her scheduled release: 100 days and counting, as she noted in one letter. She asked us to go on Craigslist and look for a good deal on an 88-key digital Yamaha piano. Misty Brooke Musick wanted to play music again! Still, Misty acknowledged herself that she sometimes experienced deep pangs of grief, though in her living environment she found it difficult to find a safe and quiet space in jail to release such vulnerable emotions.

"You can have and express <u>any</u> and <u>all</u> your emotions you want and need to while you're with us," I wrote. "We love you and want for you to heal. Recovery takes time—we will not rush you. The pain will eventually lose its sharpness."

As part of her plea agreement, Misty also agreed to a stringent Intensive Probation after her release. Terms of that probation included:

- A daily schedule which could not be deviated from without the express permission of her probation officer.
- A surveillance officer who would watch her to make sure she was where she was supposed to be.
- A strict curfew.
- Random drug/alcohol testing, several times per week.
- Drug/alcohol abuse counseling (life skills)
- 400 hours of community service.
- Major fines and other severe consequences for any violation of those terms.

Because this probation plan was to be executed and monitored in Yavapai County, where Misty's offenses occurred and where she was jailed, we had to seek permission for Misty to live in our home in Wickenburg, in Maricopa County, and to transfer the probation tracking there. Buddy got things started on that front. Everything seemed to be coming together for Misty to come home!

Misty's letter dated September 6 reflected her positive outlook:

> Ma!
>
> It's 3 a.m., and I just climbed up onto my bunk. After work, the unit officer allowed me to stay in the Day Room to complete my yoga practice before showering. It was so peaceful—the lights were dim and the concrete was cool and smooth beneath my feet. I got lost in my practice and after an hour my body relaxed into a child's pose and I felt the hand of God reach inside me and touch my heart. I heard, 'Baby Girl, stop asking why. That's for me to worry about.' Healing tears streamed down my face as I lay all alone on the Day Room floor. What a gift. I feel happy and peaceful.

I certainly hoped she could stay wrapped in that peaceful state for the last two or three months of her time in jail. Then I was reminded that this was still Misty, the woman steadfastly determined to live life on her terms.

> 10/6/14
>
> Dear Mom,
>
> So, it's been a rough day. I f----ed up and got rolled up. I'm in lockdown in G Dorm for the next 3 days. After talking with the officer who had to free me and move me over, the sergeant said I can take my old spot at the end of the 3 days and have my old job back. I'm so nervous that it won't happen and my release date will change. I cried harder today than I have in quite awhile.

You probably want to know what I did. A (male) kitchen worker sent me a note. Feeling flattered and bored, I wrote back. The a-hole kept the evidence! It's my fault—I know better. Right at the home stretch too. Please pray for me.

Three days later the issue had still not been resolved. Misty noted that it was October 9, exactly one year since she had entered county jail. In her letter to me on that date she wrote:

It's very difficult to describe how I feel right now. I suppose I'm sad and resigned to just going with the flow. I feel like an idiot for breaking the rules. I can't get away with anything, I swear! I've been such a good girl, and let me tell you that there are drugs, tattooing and sex in these dorms. This is the first thing I've done wrong. It wasn't even a scandalous note. Ugh. Deep breath. I am exactly where I'm supposed to be at this moment. "Be still and know that I am God." Breathe and trust.

A minute later she was back to daydreaming about making banana cream pies with her grandmother like she did when she was a little girl. She really did seem to have learned how to roll with the ebb and flow of life, rather than retreating into the dark world of alcohol and drugs. She also understood that life on the outside wasn't all going to be about roasting marshmallows with her sons or riding horses in the golden sunlight with me.

"I have no clue what I'm going to do next," she admitted. "I'm scared that when I get out, I will feel like I've lost my life. I'm trying so hard to just hold onto my faith in God's plan for my life, but it's so hard. What a mess I've made."

Once again, I called upon my commitment to encourage and support my daughter throughout this long period of waiting and wondering. I pulled out pen and paper and wrote this response:

Misty,

My precious Daughter! You are suffering and I can't hold you in my arms and comfort you. I hope this letter will bring peace and hope to your weary mind, body and spirit. (You are my refuge and my shield; I have put my hope in your word. — Psalm 119:114).

God is in control—you are loved. You are valued as a precious human, Daughter, Sister, Mother, Auntie, Granddaughter, and Friend. Jesus loves you and has sent His angels to watch over you. You will be home soon, your sons will be in your arms, you have a soft comfortable bed and blankets awaiting you, there are many arms waiting to hold you—you are loved, you are valued, God is in complete control.

With love — Mom

The next few weeks passed surprisingly quickly until the letter came with the wonderful news.

12/2/14

Ma! Dad!

OMG! I am going back to the worker dorm tomorrow! Guess what that means?! I'll be home for Christmas! So excited for the smell of pine, candlelight, and Christmas baking! According to my calculations, it looks like I will be out 12/17, but I will let you know for sure when the phones are re-wired.

"I'll be home for Christmas" I sang out loud as I danced around my kitchen, clutching Misty's letter. I imagined reading *The Animals' Christmas Eve* to anyone young or old who wanted to press close together to listen, singing "Happy Birthday" to Jesus and blowing out the candles, belting out *Silent Night* with Misty's voice that melts like butter leading us, and stopping to express our deep gratitude at having her back within our midst.

117

And then I would finally be able to put down my pen and paper. My daughter would be right there with me, in flesh and blood, where I could hug her, touch her, talk to her without limits, listen to her...and lovingly usher her into the next phase of her life. We made it!

CHAPTER 7

A Box Full of Hope, or a Sack of Empty Promises?

"NO MORE GLASS partition!" I kept saying to myself as Buddy and I drove up from Wickenburg to the Yavapai County jail that early morning in late December 2014. For fifteen months, that glass had stood between my daughter Misty and me, preventing us from coming together and melting into the warm embrace we both had been yearning for since drugs had yanked her away from us. Today she was finally going to be allowed to come out from the other side of that glass. She was going to re-enter our lives and begin the next phase of her journey, wherever that would take her. Misty Brooke Sanchez was finally free.

"Look at all those bags of stuff she's carrying!" I blurted out as Buddy and I watched through a window as Misty prepared for her release. Although she had come to this dismal place under the darkest of clouds, she had worked diligently to make it her home. She had used the time to heal and grow physically, mentally and spiritually. Even with all those letters we wrote back and forth, and my many visits to this jail, I knew that there was much I probably didn't know about what had been going on in Misty's mind, heart and soul all those days and nights behind bars. But I sensed that what she would be taking with her extended beyond the physical contents of those large black hefty bags she heaved over her shoulders.

We stepped out the door and watched her step out of the jail, the door slamming shut behind her. Bags in tow, Misty rushed into my arms, body slamming me as we tightly embraced. The two of us wept as her tearful Daddy unloaded the hefty bags from her firm grasp. After all those words we had shared in our letters, all the ways in which we had poured out our emotions, our wounds and our hopes to one another, words suddenly seemed unnecessary.

"Breakfast," I finally said wiping my tears. "We've got to get you some breakfast. There's a Denny's right up the road."

"Yes, I want to eat some real food too," Misty said. "But there's something else I need to do first. Can you take me somewhere to buy some cigarettes?"

"Cigarettes?" I said. "Misty, you've been off cigarettes all this time. Why would you want to start back up again?"

After a quick sideways glance, she smiled. "Cigarettes are better than other things, Mom," she said.

I had to push my frustration aside. I hadn't meant to get off on the wrong foot, but, in my mind, I added this seemingly unnecessary expense to our already stretched budget. I forced myself to let it go. There would be time, plenty of time, to discuss how Misty was going to take this new freedom and actually remain free from the demons that had come so close to ruining her life. From her jail cell she had adamantly declared that she would never submit to drug treatment unless mandated by court, but I held out hope that once she was back in the real world, with the loving nurturance of her parents and a reconnection with her three sons, she would soften that hard-line position. She had so much to live for, so much that could be sabotaged in an instant if she stumbled back into the underworld she had barely survived.

But first, it was time to honor my daughter's request. Buddy stopped to buy her cigarettes and a lighter and we began excitedly talking about plans for Misty's first few days on the outside.

"Have you been able to find the right box?" Misty asked.

"Yes, I think we've found something that will be perfect," I said. "This is going to be the best surprise ever!"

Misty and I had hatched the idea for this secret operation while she was still in jail. After breakfast and a brief stop at Janelle's, we were going to take her to Mark's home, wrapped in a giant Christmas box. We had recently purchased a large wardrobe box from one of the storage companies in town and knew it was roomy enough for Misty to stand up inside.

Mark, who was still at work, strategized with Misty over the timing of our arrival. He would inform Carlos, Brendon and Josiah only that "Papa and Grandma are coming up with an early Christmas gift." We would have the box and the present inside carefully stationed next to the boys' Christmas tree before they entered the living room.

I had taken the oversized red bow off the box so it wouldn't blow away or get crushed during transit, but once we got Misty tucked in place, with the bottom cut out of the box, I tied that bow back in position on top of the beautiful Christmas wrapping that concealed the basic cardboard box. Our cell phone cameras at the ready, it was time for lights, camera, and action!

"Okay, boys, you can come out now. Time to see what we've got for you," I announced, and as they elbowed each other for position I added, "Now this year Papa and I have really spoiled you and bought you a very, very nice gift. But you have to agree to share it!"

They eagerly ripped apart all the wrapping paper, and when they seemed just a little confused about how to open the box from the top I offered them a hint or two. Carlos backed off just a step, which I found out later was not because he was the oldest and wanted the little guys to have all the fun but because he had somehow got wind of just what this big surprise might be. When their mom popped out of the box, time stood still for a millisecond. Then Misty's long and warm arms reached fully out and embraced Brendon and Josiah, with Carlos closing in to join the family hug.

Each time I replay the video of that moment, I am struck by the absolute silence, broken only by the muffled sounds of sniffling and laughter. The mother that had drifted so far away, first to the embrace of another man and then to the killing fields of heroin, had somehow found her way back into their Christmas, into their world, into their hearts. Misty was home!

The joy of that moment was not tempered by the understanding that this would not be Misty's permanent home. Mark and Misty had been embroiled in serious marital issues for quite a long time, and their communication trail during her time in jail did not appear to be leading them toward reconciliation. At least the boys did have their mother available to them again, and they could actively dream of a lot more hugs, laughter, talks and just sharing all the little things from their everyday lives.

After this first Christmas surprise, it was time for Misty to head off with Buddy and I to what would be her temporary home—the same home she had known since she and all the Musicks became the First Family in Wickenburg to receive a Habitat for Humanity house almost twenty years earlier. Buddy had been hard at work creating a special space for Misty. He had spruced up the guest room, which would become her bedroom for however long she would stay with us. He also painted the guest bathroom, which featured new shower curtains and a full supply of Misty's favorite hygiene products that her sister Shannon had lovingly selected. It was a little like preparing for the arrival of a newborn baby, which somehow seemed to fit the occasion. My baby girl was coming home!

Misty cried and embraced Buddy when she took in the love and care he had shown with his preparations and my own heart was full to bursting. That night I felt immense gratitude just knowing that my daughter was safe in our home, sleeping in a warm comfortable bed with soft, clean sheets and fluffy pillows, instead of sleeping on the floor of her jail cell or crawling in darkened alleys in the midst of a drug run.

"It's almost surreal," I whispered to Buddy in the darkness of our own bedroom. "Misty is really here. It's just so hard to believe."

Yet it *was* real. With each new shared activity, I was reminded that Misty was definitely within our midst. We had that first cup of coffee together. We fulfilled a promise I had made during her time in jail to take her to our favorite hair salon for a mother-daughter cut and style. Misty had always taken great pride in caring for her skin and hair, at least until drugs turned everything in her life dirty and messy. That didn't matter now, though, and as I watched Misty carefully choose her new look I knew that I was glimpsing a window into this broad new experience for her. In many ways, my daughter was going to be searching out a whole new identity beyond the life she had known as wife, mother and nurse and, hopefully, light years beyond who she was while hooked on heroin, meth and booze.

"I don't even know how to dress anymore," she said during one of those early days of self-exploration. "I won't be wearing slacks and business jackets since I'm not going to be a professional. But what *should* I wear?"

In a way, she was really asking herself this question: Who am I? As the days and weeks went by, I would watch her try on a persona that featured a black leather jacket and pricey Rockabilly clothing. When that didn't seem to fit, she experimented with Western clothes and boots, which was appropriate for ranch work and riding horses in Wickenburg. Somehow, though, that wasn't it, either. She was beginning to recognize that the process of discovering who this "new Misty" was, in physical appearance and in dozens of other realms of life, was going to take time and careful consideration.

Meanwhile, Christmas had come and the entire Musick family was on hand to surround Misty in love and celebration: Brian and Heather with their son Ayaden and daughter Alexis; Shannon and Brent with baby Emmett; Janelle and Travis; our youngest son Josh; and Michael, who had no idea that Misty was home. He flew in with his Daughter Capri from their home in Tennessee. We hid Misty in one of the bedrooms and videotaped the moment he stepped into the guest room and saw her lying on the bed. It was a joyous reunion full of tears and laughter. Of course Misty's three boys and Mark was there also. Thankfully, someone videotaped the family gathered around the piano to sing *Silent Night.* In the video you can hear Misty's beautiful Alto voice rising above ours and you can see her face glowing. We were just so happy to be together, sharing our love and the spirit of what had always been such a precious holiday to us all. As Misty would happily report in a message to her out-of-state friend Sarah "It was the best f---ing Christmas ever!"

Shannon and Janelle were already in conversation with Misty to plan a Sisters' Night to relive happier days and get more up-to-date on what was happening for each of them now. During this peaceful time, there didn't seem to be any dramatic lingering effects of the strained words that had passed among them after Misty had hit rock bottom. I felt a luxurious tranquility as I basked in the warmth of my family.

I was also touched by Misty's idea for temporary employment. She knew that good jobs were going to be hard to find for a convicted felon with a drug history. Her nursing license was long gone and her criminal record would most likely be a roadblock against any attempt to resurrect her career in human resources or most other professional arenas. While she was still in jail, Misty had one idea of what she might do for the short-term.

"I had a really cool dream," she had told me. "I was working with horses."

"Well, hold onto that dream," I urged. "Let's see how we can make that happen."

So now that she was staying with us in the Roping Capital of the World, I began reaching out to my contacts. We even put a job-seeking notice up on Facebook, acknowledging her criminal record right up front. Eventually Misty found a job working for Beth, a former co-worker of mine who, with her husband, owned a large local horse and cattle ranch in Wickenburg. Misty's job would be to feed, clean horse pens and, when needed, work at roping competitions, driving steers through the chutes so they can individually burst through the gate as the riders rush in to rope them in the quickest time possible. Misty, as always, was well liked on the job. She was able to ride occasionally, although in her over-confidence she got tossed and landed on her rear just outside the arena. Fulfilling ranch duties would mean difficult physical exertion, but Misty enjoyed being active and wanted to maintain the physical stamina she had gained in jail. She worked hard and was enthusiastic about fulfilling her dream.

Yoga also had been a sustaining influence for Misty while she was behind bars. She was reminded of the need to stick with that practice when she ran into Lisa, one of her former yoga students from Yavapai County jail.

"Misty, I didn't expect to see you in Wickenburg!" Lisa said when she spotted Misty in the Circle K. Lisa had gotten out of jail a couple of months before Misty and was living with family in Wickenburg, but she had assumed that when Misty was released she would be staying in Prescott Valley. "I'll hit you up on Facebook. We've got to do yoga again," Misty told Lisa. As she walked away from that surprise meeting, Lisa was thinking of Misty's classes in jail.

"Misty was leading groups three times a week," she recalls. "She always talked about the need to find your strength, to locate the inner teeth within ourselves, and to focus on what we could accomplish and where we were going. She was adamant that she would stay sober, and she believed yoga would be a big part of that. At the end of each class she had all of us put our heads together and imagine that we were getting physically, mentally and spiritually stronger every day. Then she directed us in a breathing exercise: breathe in one word naming something you wanted in your life, breathe out one word for something you did not want in your life. For her it was inhale 'sober', exhale 'relapse.' Each person had their turn to speak out loud the words they chose for themselves. That exercise was very helpful for me."

Even outside of these groups, Misty had served as a mother figure to many inmates like Lisa. She was always eager to share information about addiction that she had learned, or discuss a new idea from the books she was reading, to help each woman understand the changes they were going through. Misty also openly talked about her personal story of how she wound up in Yavapai County jail only months after launching a nursing career as the first step toward becoming a doctor. Bumping into Misty unexpectedly gave Lisa an instant boost in her own confidence in staying clean.

Misty also was spending more time with her sons in those first few weeks after moving in with us. Mark brought them down to stay with us as often as possible, and Buddy and I had prepared one of our bedrooms for them to share during their stay. So many changes were lining up in ways that filled this mother's heart with encouragement and hope....

Oh, how I wish I could say that all these positive signs continued to point Misty in the right direction. That is the story I always wanted to tell, that my daughter's time with us would serve as a springboard toward something new, something healthy, something that would lift her up and inspire others like Lisa that were waging their own battles against the demons of drugs. But that, unfortunately, is not the story that I am able to share with you.

The storm clouds began rolling in when Misty chose to spend time visiting someone from her ex-husband Brad's family who still lived near us. When she came home, it was clear that she had been drinking beer and most likely smoking weed. When I tried to remind her again that clean and sober meant no drugs *and* no booze, she just shrugged.

"Clean and sober, that's different for me," she said. "Maybe your definition is true in your world, Mom, but in my world it's okay to drink. I'm just not going back to drugs."

Well, that declaration brought back the familiar knot tightening in my stomach. I didn't argue with her because I knew that I would always lose that argument. At least she was not trying to violate my strict rule of no alcohol our home. That was true for awhile anyway.

What happened next still makes me shudder at the reminder of how disappointed I was with the arrangements for Misty's sentencing and probation. As I mentioned earlier, the judge never listened to our desperate cry to include mandated drug treatment for Misty in their decisions in her case. And now, with the question of how she would fulfill her mandatory hours of community service, the answer left us all scratching our heads. Misty was approved to work at the Wickenburg Elk's Lodge, where she would work washing dishes, and as...a bartender!

"But, Mom, I don't drink when I'm bartending," Misty explained when I brought up how crazy this idea sounded for a woman trying to stay out of contact with booze and drugs. "Bartenders are not allowed to do that. They have very strict ethics."

Again, I didn't argue. I understood that opportunities for community service for any convicted felon were hard to come by in our little community. When I asked Pastor Duane if Mount Hope church could accommodate people like Misty by offering community service positions there, he said that in fact he used to do that. Unfortunately, the felons who spent their hours at the church abused the system by stealing computers and other costly equipment. Understandably, he had to draw the line. As I was learning, not many people are willing to give felons a second chance. I backed off on my objections...until the day I found beer bottles under Misty's bed.

"What are these doing here, Misty?" I demanded.

"Oh, well, I was at the Elk's Lodge cleaning up late one night when I came across these empty bottles," she explained. "I had already closed up so I thought it was easier if I just took them back here. I was going to get rid of them today."

"Uh-huh," I nodded. "You've been drinking in my house, that's what's happening. You know my rules. Misty, you shouldn't be drinking at all, but those are choices you have to make. I know that you're an adult. But the no-drinking rule in my home still stands. No more!"

She agreed, and that issue at least didn't come up anytime soon. However, as for the part about not drinking at all, my daughter wasn't exactly making the kinds of choices that would support a sober lifestyle. It didn't take long for this woman with a long history of toxic relationships with men to hook up with another guy who liked to drink. This time her "friend" happened to be someone our family had once known and trusted; a tattoo artist friend of our Son Michael.

It seemed to begin innocently enough with Chris's offer to help us out. Misty was required to report for regular urine analysis tests, on short notice. That meant quick trips to Phoenix, more than an hour away. Buddy had been driving her most of the time, but it was tiring for him. He was still struggling with the effects of the autoimmune disorder that had brought him to the Mayo Clinic during Misty's jail stay.

"I live out that way, so I can come get you and take you back and forth, no problem," Chris told Misty.

Well, I could see that Chris was attracted to Misty, as so many men were, and my radar was bleeping "Danger! Danger!" Once again, however, I did not interfere. It was Misty's life, and anything to lessen the burden on my husband was difficult to refuse. I decided that I would wait and watch whether this storm cloud might blow over until….

It was dark, hours after Chris should have brought Misty home one night, when I finally called him and left a message.

"Chris, we have placed our trust in you. We need to know where our daughter is," I said. Minutes later, Misty called back.

"Misty where are you? What's going on?" I asked, my fear rising in all too familiar ways.

"Mom, I'm going to be honest with you. We've been drinking," she said.

"You what? Misty, you belong home. You're supposed to be clean and sober. What if your Parole Officer stops by here? I would have to tell her where you're at and you'd be in serious trouble."

"Mom, this is not a big deal," she said. "We're just going to spend the night out here and I'll be back early tomorrow morning."

She did come back, as promised, but I knew I couldn't stand by while this arrangement continued. And since Chris had been a friend of the family, I went directly to him to speak my peace. He admitted that he had been buying Misty booze for awhile and that they had become involved. He insisted that he was falling in love with her and that it wasn't my place to get in the way.

"She is an adult, you know," he said coldly.

"But you can't treat an addict like you would other adults," I said, trying to stay calm. "In some respects they are like children. And what you're doing with Misty is really disrespecting us, working against what we are trying to do for her. She's not just an alcoholic; she's also a drug addict."

"You know what? If she's going to use, she's going to use, whether it's with me or somebody else," he insisted. "At least I really love her and care about what happens to her."

"No, you are trying to steal what we're trying to save!" I shouted.

I was the lioness again, re-awakening the role I had played as Misty's protector years and years earlier. Yes, Misty absolutely shared the blame for what was happening, but if I couldn't get through to her on matters like this at least I could try to block the path of someone intruding on her territory. As it turned out, Chris cooled on the relationship. I'm not sure I was the only influence, however. Evidence would suggest that Misty did not share in Chris's vision of an exclusive, permanent love relationship.

Misty was not through with men, not by a long shot. And temptations were steadily closing in on her. As time went by this would become increasingly more evident. It had already revealed itself one day when she came home from the ranch with startling news.

"Mom, the kid they just hired at the ranch is a heroin addict and I'm stressing out!" she exclaimed.

"What? Are you sure?" I asked. The question I wanted to ask was "and are you using?" But I was convincing myself that Misty and the needle would never reunite again.

"Heroin addicts just know each other. I can see him spending an extended amount of time in the bathroom, and when he comes out he's got blood on his sleeve."

"Oh no! What are you going to do to protect yourself, Misty?"

"I'll tough it out, Mom. Don't worry, I'll be okay."

Later that week, Misty added even more frightening details to the scene. She had allowed this young man to use her phone to do business, which meant that he was calling his dealers and leaving a trail of "dirty" phone numbers on her cell. When she insisted that she would take care of that and everything would be fine, my heart dropped to the floor.

Soon my daughter began coming home from work dragging her feet, rather than carrying that bounce in her step that I had grown accustomed to seeing. "I'm just not feeling well," Misty moaned. This was another occasion when alarm bells should have been sounding in my brain, but I was still naïve and too trusting. In reality, a short time after her "'illness," she actually admitted to me that she had used heroin with that co-worker, and, in reality she had become dope sick, which means she was detoxing from the heroin.

"Yes, I had a relapse," she said. "But, Mom, you should be really proud of me—I threw all my syringes and other paraphernalia away. I don't want to go back to that stuff. I'm not going back, Mom. I'm not."

"Sweetie, I really am proud of you," I said. "I'm also very concerned. You really need to be getting some help."

"Mom, I'm going to be fine," she said. "I'm doing just what I'm supposed to be doing."

I did see her re-reading some of those inspirational books she had turned to in jail. More important to me, I knew she was reading her Bible. Of course I believed that she really needed the structure, accountability and comradeship of a recovery program, but she was a strong-willed woman who had made it clear to me on so many occasions that she would not be pushed.

I held out hope that living in our protected home environment could still provide her the inner strength to go back to making the right kinds of choices. Addicts relapse, I reminded myself. It's part of the terrain. Roy had tried and failed eight times before getting clean. Misty was back on her feet for now. Let's see what happens next.

Buddy and I weren't the only ones closely watching Misty's behavior and worrying about her choices. Her sons were continuing to spend extended periods of time with their mom at our home, and the routine was not living up to the images they had carried in their minds while she was in jail.

"We had so many great plans about what we would do together when she got out," recalls Carlos, who had just turned fifteen when Misty was released. "We would go to Jump Street and other places around Phoenix. We'd go back to the rivers we used to play in when I was younger. We'd go dirt-bike riding, or just have a cup of coffee or tea together early in the morning before she went to work."

Oh, but as Misty's oldest son would so sadly discover, those expectations were a far cry from reality. Misty's restrictions kept her from driving, and she showed no real desire to take her boys on those fun outings anyway. And her attitude when she was around Carlos and his two brothers simply didn't convey that same spirit they felt on the wonderful day when she had popped out of that giant Christmas box.

"She was there but she wasn't a hundred percent there," Carlos said of his time with Misty in our home. Carlos was mature enough to understand Misty's drug history and temptations. And since Misty had vowed to be honest with her son, she admitted to him when she began using again. That put Carlos and his brothers in a position no child should ever have to bear.

"Instead of being outside having fun, we would be inside watching her closely and being very careful around her," he explains. "If she didn't get home from work when she was supposed to, I would get suspicious and scared. I felt like every single hour that we were there, we were turning more and more into adults. When she told me that she had used drugs again, I said, 'Mom, you have to stop this! This is why you were in jail!' I was speaking from my heart, but she wasn't taking my words into her heart."

Over time, Misty's visits with her sons would become shorter and less frequent. That box full of hope that the boys had opened on that pre-Christmas day was beginning to turn into a dirty sack full of empty promises.

Now, I can't be sure on the sequence of things that happened over the late winter and spring of 2015. The order of events wasn't making much sense when they were tumbling one over the other as they came along, and they still don't make sense to me today. Unfortunately, I do remember the consequences of far too many experiences that I wish I could forget.

I recall Misty telling me that Johnny, her "friend" from jail, was about to be released and that she wanted to go back to Yavapai County to see him. Johnny wasn't from Arizona. Around jail he was referred to as "Arkansas," his home state. He worked in the kitchen at the jail—apparently he was the one who had slipped Misty a note, leading to her losing her job in the jail's laundry room for awhile. It would seem that Misty had been swapping notes with this guy for awhile, and their contact was not as innocent as she described it to me at the time. Now she was asking Buddy to drive her up there to meet him so they could spend a night at a hotel together.

"You don't really know this man," I cautioned. In my mind, as I imagined Misty engaging in sexual relations with someone who also had done time in jail for drug charges, I was flashing to images of something that I had uncovered while going through her Facebook account while she was in jail. While Misty was on her self-destructive binge soon after Rick OD'd, she got high while staying at the home of a male drug dealer and wound up getting gang-raped. When she described some of what was done to her that night, I remembered how I would care for her as a baby. Those awful things had happened to my baby girl!

"But I did get to know Johnny in jail," Misty responded, pulling me out of my panic zone. "We flirted, and he's hot, Mom. Anyway, if Dad doesn't take me up there I'll just find another way."

So I said yes, or at least I didn't say no, and Misty went up there and had her little visit with this guy Johnny until Buddy drove him to the airport to head back to Arkansas. Whew! That was one storm cloud that had passed. Or so I thought. A few weeks later Misty came to me with a proposal.

"Mom, what would you and Dad say if Johnny came to live here with us?" she asked. "It's not working for him at home with his family, and Mom, he's trying to live for the Lord. He wants to keep his life straight and I know I can help him."

"Are you kidding me?" I asked. "You want to live with another convicted felon…under our roof?"

"Mom," she said, more seriously, "I'm a grown woman. This is what I want to do. I need love in my life if I'm going to keep moving forward. If you don't agree to this, I'll just ask Grandma if she will keep him over at her place, or I'll work something out with someone else."

And that's what got to me. Today, I know that Misty was manipulating me and I was going right along for the ride. I got caught up in worrying about how this arrangement would turn out if Misty had to keep it clandestine. At least if they were both in my home, I could keep my eyes on them and hopefully be of some positive influence. After all, it was when Misty was far away, and mostly out of touch, that she had gotten sucked into the downward spiral a couple of years earlier. So that's how I came to allow Johnny to seek permission from his own probation officer to live in our home, in a room separate from Misty's, and otherwise say "yes" to a plan that anyone looking at from the outside would immediately scream "No!"

Johnny was a pleasant guy, with a nice sense of humor, and from what I heard he, like Misty, had been popular among his fellow inmates. I could see how he and Misty might fit together. Buddy and I did our best to communicate our expectations for this living arrangement, and we were encouraged when we would see them reading their Bible together and talking about the recovery process. They seemed sincere, at least from what I could see…or perhaps from what I wanted to see.

Misty continued working at the ranch and kept up her community service at the Elk's Lodge. For awhile, our in-house arrangement of two ex-convicts and drug addicts trying their best to toe the line seemed like it could work. Of course, I didn't catch wind of an incident when Misty and Johnny visited Shannon and Brent, and Misty asked her sister to use her urine to pass a mandatory drug test. "I had a kidney stone and had to take a Percocet for it," Misty explained. Shannon didn't buy it, but apparently Misty was turning to other little tricks that she had learned to pass her UA's.

Still, Misty and Johnny appeared to be doing well in their relationship. That's why I was surprised when I noticed he was spending longer periods of time away. I was not his parent or his probation officer, but I did have a stake in his well-being because he was going to have a major impact on my daughter. Johnny seemed to suddenly avoid interacting with Buddy and me.

"So where's Johnny these days?" I asked Misty innocently.

"Oh, he went up to the Valley," she explained.

"Really, who does he know there?"

"Oh, just people he met when he was in jail. He's doing some work for a local contractor. He needs to make some money."

When Johnny did come "home," I noticed that his eyes were glassy and his pupils were enlarged. Buddy had told me earlier that when Johnny first came to stay with us, he had lost weight since the day Buddy had left him at the airport to go back to Arkansas. Hmm.

"Can I talk to you outside for a moment?" I asked Johnny. When I got him out there I asked directly, "Johnny, what are you on?"

"Ma'am, I'm not gonna lie to you. I'm on meth," he said.

"What? We can't have two addicts relapsing in this house. You have got to get treatment."

It didn't take long to learn the rest of the story of Johnny and meth. The reason he had first come to Arizona, and wound up in jail so far from home, is that he was involved with transporting meth over state lines. He was a drug dealer...and he was living in my house! The storm clouds had circled all around me, and I had no idea where to turn for cover.

Misty and Johnny both swore they would go to NA meetings. I believe they went to a total of two. They did go back to reading the Bible and would at least talk about taking the steps toward recovery, and for a period of time they appeared to be making some progress. Then came the morning when Misty and Johnny were wandering aimlessly around our front yard. Misty told me that while she and Johnny were being intimate, she saw someone crouched on the wall outside their window staring inside.

"What? How long ago did this happen?" I asked.

"I don't know, like maybe thirty minutes ago," Misty said with a trace of the slurring I had heard in her voice before.

I called the police myself and in a few minutes several cruisers were swarming our house while officers frantically searched outside. Meanwhile, Misty and Johnny hid in Misty's room. Nothing or no one was discovered.

"I did tell your dispatcher that this happened thirty minutes ago," I explained sheepishly. Soon the annoyed cops were gone, and Buddy and I were huddling about what to do with our two house guests. It was clear that they had been delusional with their report of a prowler, and that was a sure sign of meth use. My daughter and her boyfriend were doing hard drugs in my house! We had considered writing up a strict contract for the terms under which Misty and Johnny could stay with us earlier but had not yet acted on that. I knew now that we had to give them an ultimatum: total sobriety in our home, or get out.

Before we could decide how and when to approach Misty and Johnny, I walked into their guest bathroom early the next morning and found fecal material and vomit splattered on and around the toilet. When I confronted Misty, she made no attempt to lie herself out of this one.

"Mom, we're dope sick," she said. "We're detoxing cold turkey."

"Misty, you go right in there and get Johnny's butt out of bed," I said. "At nine o'clock sharp we are all having a meeting outside."

They did show up, but Johnny was slurring his words and as I looked at my daughter I could see that her entire face was covered with red pocks. I knew right then that they were in serious trouble. We were *all* in serious trouble.

"I've had enough!" I shouted. "You two desperately need to be in treatment, but I can't control that. What I can control is what is happening in my home. We have been giving you an opportunity to start living a clean and decent life by staying here, but through your actions you are totally disrespecting us. No more. I have written a contract that says that you must stay clean and sober here. If you don't, you will need to leave immediately."

Since we were outside and my voice was escalating, the neighbors soon picked up on what was going on.

"Tweakers! F---ing tweakers!" a voice called out. It was the neighbor next door that had offered Misty and Johnny beer and weed. This same person was now mocking her and Johnny for being "tweakers," a well-known drug world term for meth addicts. Johnny shouted back to him and suddenly Brian pulled up in front of our house. I had called to tell him what was happening and he was completely fed up with their behavior. So now Brian was screaming at them to get their act together, Misty was crying and Johnny was slurring excuses. It was a loud fiasco, and Brian became angry when I asked him to stop. In the midst of the turmoil, it suddenly occurred to me just how badly addictions disrupt the serenity of home and family. I'm sure the entire neighborhood was tuning into the scene—just as I used to watch out my window when young people would line up with their backpacks waiting for their drug drop-offs. The dirty, crazy, dangerous drug underworld had circled around and landed right on us!

As the shouting subsided, all I really cared about was whether or not these two struggling addicts were going to sign our contract.

"We'll have to think about this," Misty said, but before night had fallen they had signed. The calm after the storm settled in, and at one point Misty actually chose to take advantage of the no-cost rehabilitation services offered through the Salvation Army. Johnny declined to join her, though he did drive her there. Misty made it clear to us that she did not want us as a family to be involved in anything that she would do there. Still, it was a start.

And it lasted just two weeks. Johnny drove her back home. I didn't want to show any anger or frustration this time. I was trying to keep my head together without revealing the near panic I felt inside.

"I think I know why you didn't stay in treatment," I said softly. "You already lost one boyfriend to an overdose while you were away in treatment and you're afraid that if you stay in treatment now, you'll lose another boyfriend the same way."

Momentarily startled, Misty nodded slightly before looking away, muffling her sobs. Was she really forfeiting her own chances for recovery in the name of "saving" this new boyfriend? She might have believed this was love, just as she had believed she was in love with Rick, but it was really her addiction distorting her thinking. If she sincerely cared for Johnny and wanted to help save his life, wouldn't she press forward by embracing recovery and continue to encourage him to do the same? In more ways than I would care to admit to myself, Misty was repeating so much of what had happened with the lover that she had turned to when she ran away from her husband and children. In fact, as I would discover later, Misty had introduced Johnny to heroin, just as Rick had introduced the needle to Misty. That's what the demons of drug addiction do to you: they get you churned up in their dangerous and destructive behavior, they chew you up and spit you out, and then rinse and repeat.

I only hoped that this time around, the outcome would be different. I just didn't know how. Oh sure, I can look back from the wisdom and understanding of today and say, "Crap! I should have turned Misty and Johnny into their probation officers the second I knew they had used drugs again." Misty would have been better off in jail because she was powerless over her addiction in her current life situation. I was powerless, too. I tried hard not to enable my daughter, taking what I knew from my profession and doing my best to work with my husband, who was not always on the same page. "Let's wait" he would say to my suggestions for tough love. I did my own research on treatment options for Misty—and for Johnny if he chose to come along. I was convinced that she would have the best chance of climbing the mountain of recovery with Teen Challenge USA, the faith-based program for adolescents and adults that had established an excellent success record in facilitating recovery for addicts all over the country.

Ah, but Misty had her own ideas. To her credit, she and Johnny did appear to be actively researching their options. In fact, she was carrying a folder of drug-treatment information one morning when she knocked on our bedroom door and walked in.

"Mom and Dad, we have a found a place for us to go together," she announced in a professional tone. "All we need is a hundred fifty dollars to get us started."

Well, I was done giving my daughter money. Buddy and I already had handed over a great deal of money for her legal fees, her gas money and her housing needs, while she sent money to pay off Johnny's car so he could get to Arizona. Meanwhile, the roping season had come to an end and Misty was no longer needed at her ranch job. I'm sure that much of the money she earned got channeled right into drug deals. Maybe that's what this $150 she was asking for now was all about. There had been so much secrecy and lies that I no longer trusted either of them.

"How about we pay you half and you go and have a talk with Pastor Duane about the other half?" I suggested.

In response, Misty abruptly closed her folder.

"Well, I guess that's that," she said. "I don't know what else to do."

I asked her about going back to Salvation Army, and I brought up Teen Challenge one more time. She just shook her head.

"That's not where Johnny wants to go," she said, "and we will not be separated."

Buddy even offered to take Misty and Johnny to the treatment center of their choice and hand the money she was requesting directly to the program director.

"No, we want to do this on our own," she said.

After Misty walked away, I knew that I could no longer afford to sit in a stalemate. I began texting Misty's probation officer, telling the truth of the many ways my daughter had been violating the terms of her Intensive Probation.

"I would rather see my daughter in jail again than roaming the streets or being found dead of an overdose," I wrote.

The walls were closing in on Misty. Her PO advised her that she would either have to get herself back into the Salvation Army program or go to jail. Meanwhile, she showed signs of using again. She made a few excuses for missing scheduled UA's, and she was more closely guarding the backpack that I strongly suspected was holding drugs and paraphernalia. When I suggested one time that she was guarding her backpack, she moaned, "Oh, *Mom*, give me a break" and shot me one of the looks like how dare you be suspicious. I should have demanded that she open that backpack on the spot, but once again I held back. It was another example of that recurring question: What do I do now? And you almost never have a clear answer.

I kept reminding myself about our signed contract. My daughter was flaunting a concrete agreement that she had made with us, and this was our house. At last, Buddy and I calmly but firmly confronted our beloved daughter about violating her contract. Either she would choose sobriety, which meant entering treatment right now, or she would need to leave our home.

"Well, I knew this was coming," Misty sputtered.

And she was gone.

At first she stayed alone in a dark, dumpy Wickenburg motel just up the road from our warm, cozy home. She was hardly eating. Johnny, back working for that contractor, or so he said, apparently wired her some money to keep her afloat. Buddy brought her some food, and with a tear in his eye he told me about her gaunt appearance. We were on edge, constantly terrified of what may happen next.

At some point Johnny returned from his job, and he and Misty disappeared together. By now it was June, around the start of summer, with the temperatures soaring over 100 degrees and the snowbirds long since having retreated to their off-season homes. Wickenburg had settled into what was for me an eerie quiet. With Misty barely communicating with us, I was left to wonder and worry about what she was doing, where she was going and what on earth was keeping her from claiming the healthy life that she had apparently chosen during her time in jail. Now she was caught in a different kind of prison: the steely jaws of addiction.

I did hear that her PO and Johnny's PO gave each of them an order of separation. Ha, they were not going to listen to that order! Were they also actively using meth and other drugs? I certainly assumed that. With Johnny presumably no longer working, were they resorting to criminal behavior to support their habits and survive on the run? I hated to imagine that, but it could well have been true. Did they have any concrete, reasonable plan of what to do next? Well, there were no signs pointing in that direction, that's for sure. Did I have moments when I feared that the next news I would hear about my daughter was that she was…dead? I tried to pretend that those fears were not following me, but they were, like boiling lava threatening to erupt.

I vowed to go on with my life, though. Some days I would roam the streets of Wickenburg hoping to see the little green car she and Johnny were driving, or to stumble upon other clues. It was as if the hands of the clock had been turned back twenty years and Misty had just broken her teenage curfew. I wasn't getting anywhere, and of course I had no way of knowing whether she was anywhere near our town. She could have been in Phoenix or back near Prescott Valley or halfway to some far-off place for all I knew.

We didn't know it at the time, but during those days Misty was occasionally reaching out to old friends from her drugging days in Prescott Valley. "I'm dabbling in it again and I think I've pushed it too far," she wrote to one friend. To another she confided, "I have definitely gotten myself into a mess. Sitting in a parking lot in Phoenix right now waiting on a weird dealer dude to take me to a place I can stay a few nights. Need to get out of the state immediately but have no money. I will be hustling tomorrow but it's so risky."

Those are messages we didn't find until it was much too late. We asked the police to search that cheap Wickenburg motel she had been staying at, in case she had gone back, but there was no sign of her there. Then I remembered that Lisa, Misty's friend in jail who lived in town, had been working with Misty for awhile at the Elk's Lodge. Maybe she might know something.

Buddy called Lisa, and as we would only discover much later, Misty was actually right there waving her hand in a motion that clearly said, "Don't tell them I'm here." Lisa did as Misty asked. It was always hard to say no to Misty, especially for anyone who cared about her. And I know Lisa cared deeply for my daughter. She had actually cooked Misty and Johnny a dinner of fresh salmon, vermicelli and salad and held Misty while she was dope sick. Lisa hoped that Misty was getting over the hump—that she would get back on the recovery trail, that she would start leading those yoga classes that she had promised Lisa she would get going again when they had bumped into each other around Christmas but never did. Lisa desired the same thing we longed for— to see Misty in recovery.

Unfortunately, the evidence before Lisa's eyes told her something different. Johnny was out for two hours "buying cigarettes" and when he came back Misty locked herself in the bathroom, coming out with fresh needle marks. "I'm going to have to ask you guys to leave," Lisa said. Misty asked for money and started babbling about how they needed to get fake IDs and that they were going "someplace no one could ever find them." Lisa handed Misty $82, which was all the money she had. Misty was a friend....

The days of early July are all just a blur to me now. I know I kept up frantic contact with Misty's PO, who now had no-shows as well as dirty and diluted UA's on Misty's record. I made call after call to Johnny's cell phone because Misty apparently didn't have one anymore. At one point we had at least a glimmer of optimism: Misty's PO believed that Misty was going to listen to the ultimatum of getting treatment or going back to jail and was making some sort of plan to report, possibly back to the Salvation Army or maybe somewhere else. On the Wednesday this was supposed to happen, I was bouncing all over my house waiting for confirmation that Misty had come to her senses and was taking a step in the right direction. But that confirmation call never came. Finally, I dialed Johnny's number one more time.

"What's going on? I haven't heard from you guys. Is Misty in treatment? Why haven't you called me?" I asked.

"No, she's not in treatment," he said when I finally took a break from peppering him with questions. "But I promised Misty that I would not talk to you about this. She has to be the one to talk to you."

"Then put her on the line!" I shouted.

"She's not here right now, but she will call you...sometime tonight."

This was one time that Misty kept her word. She called me soon afterward.

"Mom, I just want you to know—" she began, but I cut her off.

"Sweetie, what's going on? I thought you were going to treatment. And you haven't reported to your PO," I stammered.

"I'm not going to treatment, and I'm not going back to the PO. I've made my decision. We are going to do this our way," she said in that firm, resolute voice that I had come to dread.

"What? Are you friggin' kidding me? Have you completely lost your mind? You're telling me that you're just going to become fugitives and keep running from the law?"

"That's correct, Mom. I'm sorry that you don't agree with my decision, but this is my life."

"But, what about your family? What about your boys?"

"Mom, they're going to be okay."

"Misty, I cannot support this. No, you can't...you have to report to your PO. If you have to go back to prison at least you'll be safe there and...Misty, what are you going to do out on your own running from the law? Where will you go?"

"I don't know. Maybe we'll go to Mexico...or something."

"No, you can't....I just can't accept this."

"Well, I love you Mom."

I paused for a moment, rehearsing in my mind my next desperate argument. But then I immediately heard Misty's likely response in my mind, and I let it go.

"I love you, too," I said, my words tinged with displeasure and sarcasm. Surrendering to my daughter's crazy, drug-clouded ideas and explanations in that moment did not feel like love, at least not the way I believed love should work. My love was supposed to be strong enough to sway my daughter during her darkest and most troubled hour. My love was supposed to mean never giving up.

"She's lost her mind," I said to Buddy as we lay together in bed later that night. "She's really choosing to leave her children, leave her family, and leave everything. I just cannot believe this."

Unable to sleep, I kept replaying our phone conversation in my mind. When I tried to shut those tapes off, I flashed to the words from one of Misty's favorite songs, *Lost in Paradise* by Evanescence, about running away and not feeling the pain. Then I suddenly remembered a different talk with Misty somewhere between the thrill of bringing her home from jail and the agony of hearing that she was choosing to run from it all, leading a life of constant danger and uncertainty. The talk I was recollecting was not about drugs, or recovery programs or Johnny.

"Mom, I used to be a professional woman," she was lamenting that day. "I used to wear a suit and heels and work in HR. I was highly respected. And then I was a nurse, with a great deal of responsibility. Now I'm just a pretty girl behind a bar at an Elk's Lodge. That's all I am."

"No, that's not all you are," I argued. "You are Misty. No matter what your title, no matter what job you do, you are precious, Misty. That's more important than anything."

I don't think she paid me much attention. She just could not accept that she was a beloved child of God, loved by so many people, and that her life was completely worthwhile as it was—recognizing that she had fallen and calling upon God's strength to get back up again. She didn't have to *do* anything, she only had to *be* the person she was meant to be, healthy and whole and free from drugs.

"But blessed is the one who trusts in the Lord, whose confidence is in Him. They will be like a tree planted by the water that sends out its roots by the stream." – Jeremiah 17:7.

I posted that verse on Facebook during one of those sad, frustrating days. We kept calling the police, reminding them that Misty had broken off contact with her PO while in violation of her probation terms. No warrant for her arrest had been issued yet, but they assured me they would be looking. The PO said she was doing all she could to track Misty down and move toward a resolution.

I tried Johnny's phone again, but I wasn't fooling myself into believing that he would pick up. I left a message anyway: "Well, I've heard you two are having great adventures. Know that your fun is costly to others. We as parents wonder if you're dead or alive…strung out somewhere on drugs. Understand that although this is YOUR life, your decisions are affecting others. Please consider what you are doing, Misty. At least in prison, your family, your boys, can see you. Your oldest son is angry at your choice; your middle son sleeps with his father because he's too afraid to sleep in his own bed. Please consider the messages you are sending them. I love you and I'm also feeling very frustrated."

And then I went back to waiting and hoping…and praying.

CHAPTER 8

————— ❧ —————

The Knock at the Door

I WAS SORTING through the fruits and vegetables in the Produce section of our Wickenburg Safeway that Monday afternoon in late July when a surprising sensation came over me. I was actually feeling calm and peaceful! I was even talking with people I knew and some I didn't know, part of my social nature that had been shelved in my constant worry. For the moment, I wasn't engulfed by fears of where Misty was and what was happening to her. Maybe I had found that place inside of deep trust and faith, or maybe I just needed a break from the intensity.

Wow, I haven't felt this good in a long time, I thought.

I put away the groceries, considered dinner options and headed to our bedroom to unwind for a few minutes with Buddy. "They're going to find her," I was saying softly to myself. "She will go back to prison and start over again. This time the courts will steer her toward recovery and she will recognize that it really is her time to get well. It will all be fine."

It was strange and sad to find comfort in the possibility of my daughter getting arrested, but in this mother's heart and mind, prison was a safer place than the dark streets and unlit alleys of the addict. I allowed myself to imagine a reasonably good night's sleep after a relaxing evening—as relaxed as you can ever get when your daughter is running from the law, taking drugs like meth and heroin, and living on the streets with assorted addicts and criminals.

When I heard the knock at the door, I immediately got up and walked to the kitchen. Glancing out the front window, I spotted a police cruiser. "Look, Buddy, the cops are here," I said excitedly, and then added, "They've finally found her!" Buddy was right behind me as I opened the door.

"Oh my gosh, this is about my daughter, isn't it? Did you find Misty? Where is she? Is everything okay?" I was babbling, and it was just beginning to register that it was not one police officer at our door but three. In response to my giddy enthusiasm, they looked to the side or down at their feet. I could tell by their uniforms that the older one, closest to the door, was with the Department of Public Safety, or Highway Patrol, and the two men standing a few feet behind him were local Wickenburg police officers. Those two had their hands folded in front of them, sort of like ushers at a wedding. Strange. Then my eyes caught the photo that the DPS officer was holding in his right hand with some papers. It was Misty!

"That's my daughter," I said pointing to the photo, but as I spoke he jerked the photo aside. That was strange, too.

"Ma'am, do you know Misty Sanchez?" he said clearly and calmly.

"Yes, our daughter Misty. We've been waiting to hear—"

"She's been in an accident," the officer interjected.

"Oh no!" Buddy groaned. In that moment, I could almost detect the comma in the officer's sentence, but I resisted filling in the words that would come next.

"And...it was fatal," he added.

I spun from the door. *NO!! This can't be true!!!* I thought. *Run, just run! Run far away as fast as you can to someplace where these words will not be real!*

Buddy caught me in his arms and held me with all his loving strength as a guttural scream was unleashed from deep within my abdomen, the place that once housed my tiny growing firstborn baby thirty-four years ago. My brain couldn't comprehend what the officers had just told me. My Daughter, my precious Misty was dead.

"NO! NO! NO! NO! NOT MY DAUGHTER, NOT MY DAUGHTER!!"

The words were uncontrollably spewing from my throat, the sound of my screams like the piercing death cry of an animal trapped in the jaws of its predator—a prey animal with no escape. Buddy held me tightly to keep me from running, or crumbling to the floor. I screamed for so long, I assumed the officers had left. "When things settle down, I will tell you what happened," I heard spoken in a soothing voice. I lifted my head. I wanted to know what happened to my beautiful, precious daughter. I HAD to know.

Gathering my composure, I willed myself to settle down enough to listen to each detail. The DPS officer speaking had kind eyes and spoke with compassion. He explained that Misty had perished when the minivan she was riding in crashed into the rear of a disabled tractor-trailer parked on the shoulder of the I-17 freeway by the Dixileta Bridge. The van was doing 70 or 75 miles an hour when it hit the truck and there were no brakes, so the van took the full impact. My daughter, who had been sitting without a seat belt on an unsecured love seat placed in the back of the van, was violently ejected from the side window. There was no way she could have survived her severe injuries. Johnny, who had been dozing while buckled in the front passenger seat, was killed instantly. He never knew what hit him.

When the officer explained that "a detective in an unmarked vehicle was traveling 100 feet behind the minivan when the collision occurred," I gasped.

"This is God," I found myself saying to Buddy, now standing across the island in the kitchen. I could not have articulated then why I believed that the hand of God had arranged for that detective to witness the horrible scene at 6 a.m. that day, but as time went on I would understand very clearly. I would want to know, need to know, everything that happened in the last seconds of my daughter's life. This detective who "just happened" to be there to witness this brutal scene was in a position to provide all the answers.

The driver of their minivan somehow survived. He actually stood up from a small pocket of wreckage. He was arrested at the scene and after being treated at a nearby hospital was taken to jail and charged with two counts of second degree murder. Evidence clearly pointed to the use of drugs, meth and heroin specifically, by all three passengers in that minivan.

Fortunately, the driver of the tractor-trailer, who had been sitting in his truck at the moment of impact, sustained only minor injuries. Miraculously, he had just climbed back into the cab after placing orange safety triangles behind the big rig to warn other drivers. He watched the disaster happen in horror from his side view mirror. Bewildered, he opened his door, stepped from his truck and witnessed the horrific sight of the smashed vehicle and my daughter's twisted body strewn on the pavement of the freeway.

The tragic accident had been on the news all day, but since we didn't have cable TV we were totally oblivious. I suddenly realized that the calm and peacefulness I had been experiencing at the Safeway and throughout most of that day had actually taken hold of me in the hours *after* my daughter had died.

Eventually the three officers left us alone. As Buddy and I stood in the kitchen staring into each other's eyes, I muttered, "How could it end this way?" I found my mind flashing to images of Misty and Johnny reading the Bible in our home, trying to pray. Like Misty, Johnny had his own Christian foundation and in their own way they both would turn to God to seek a way out of their pain and suffering. I had seen them struggle against the meth and heroin demons that called their names, seductively whispering their promises of relief and the bliss of oblivion. Unfortunately, Misty and Johnny never allowed Buddy and I, or almost anyone else, inside their circle of pain and torture interrupted by occasional snippets of hope. They chose to struggle and strive alone. And now their struggle was over. They were gone. I thought of my daughter growing up, playing the piano, singing, erupting in laughter, and the pain was so great I thought my chest would burst.

We quickly turned to our cell phones to track news of the accident. Stories and photos were everywhere. I couldn't bear to hold my gaze for more than a second on most of the visual images, but in one photo of the wreckage scene I noted the yellow tarp to the left of the mini-van, and then a shoe nearby.

"That's Misty's shoe!" I gasped, and, at that very moment it occurred to me that the tarp I was looking at was covering my dead daughter. I didn't have the time or the stomach to linger over any more accounts of the crash. It was time to get on the phone.

Brian and Heather lived the closest, so when I contacted them I told them only that they needed to drive to our home so Buddy and I could share some urgent news with them. "It's not about your dad," Heather said to Brian, who had been worrying about Buddy's health. "Your mom would have been able to tell you about that on the phone."

Before they arrived, I made the difficult calls to Janelle and Travis, and to Michael in Tennessee. Janelle and Misty had so much history, and I know how sad she would be to finally lose forever the sister she had watched slipping away for years. Michael had been the one who proclaimed that once a person gets hooked on heroin they don't usually come back, but now he was just devastated like all of us who loved Misty.

When I called Shannon and Brent's home, I knew that Josh, our youngest, was staying there while he sorted out his next moves after graduating from high school. While on speaker phone, Shannon mumbled "that sucks." Then I heard the sound of Josh's agonizing screams in the background: "No! No! No!" He was wildly flailing his arms, slamming them against the walls. I took the phone from my ear so I wouldn't have to listen to the full intensity of his screams.

"Mom, I need to hang up. We've got to take care of Josh," Shannon said.

When I called Mark, I could tell that the news had hit him just as hard. Although Misty had hurt him badly, he still loved her. He assured me that he was there for the three boys, holding them tight during this tornado. I had absolutely no doubt that his love, caring and protection of Misty's three sons would never waiver as they faced a life without their mother.

Buddy had not screamed when the cops knocked on our door, focusing all his energy on supporting me. A few days later, however, I would hear his gasping sobs. I knew there was nothing I could do to soothe him. He had lost his baby girl forever.

I posted the news on Facebook because so many dear friends had been following Misty's battle with addiction and had offered us their prayers and support during these last frantic weeks. The public responses and private messages that followed reminded me that I was loved, and that Misty had been loved by so many. It wasn't just *our* tragedy....

David's Desert Chapel Funeral Home was just outside the center of Wickenburg. As I stepped inside the entrance with Buddy, Mark and Pastor Duane, I nodded as I read the words of the sign: "When Someone You Love Becomes a Memory, Your Memory Becomes a Treasure." David Poyner, the owner, greeted us warmly in the reception area and, after offering his condolences, he began to go over the arrangements for the cremation. We selected a beautiful urn to hold Misty's ashes and then moved to another room with sample-sized caskets and cardboard boxes attached to the wall. As I listened to the others discussing the small brown cardboard box designated for use in the crematory, I gasped and struggled to breathe: how could my daughter's body be squished into something so tiny? I didn't understand that these were but samples and that the box for the cremation would be full size. Pastor Duane protectively put his arm over my shoulders and ordered everyone to stop until I could regain my composure.

A few minutes later, we were back in the safety of the reception area. That's when David looked me in the eye from across the table and began explaining something that was not at all what I had been expecting.

"I'm going to give your family a discount and I'll tell you why," he said. "I knew your daughter Misty and I have a question in my heart. If I had made another choice in dealing with her, could things possibly have turned out differently?"

David happened to have been Misty's boss at the Elk's Lodge, where she was fulfilling her mandatory hours of community service.

One day he discovered a $300 shortfall. The alarm system had indicated when someone had come in after hours, and that person had carefully shut the system off and turned it back on. When David explained all this to Misty, he told her that he was asking everyone on staff if they knew anything about it.

"I did it," Misty admitted. "I do really stupid things when I'm on drugs."

David was surprised. Before that moment he had considered Misty to be an honest, hard-working bartender whom he often called "a super employee." He knew her history, but as far as he could determine she had not touched a drop of alcohol that she served and watched over. When Misty cried and told him that she was going to report to rehab in two days, he held her hand. He was convinced that she really wanted to get herself together.

"I won't report you because I know they will send you right back to jail," he said. "After rehab you can come back here and work off the money. But Misty, you have got to find new friends to hang around. If you don't get your sh-t together, you're going to end up in my cooler."

And now, only a couple of weeks later, there she was, down the hall, lying broken in his cooler.

"I feel guilty. I should have turned her in," he said, fighting back tears. "But the most striking thing is that she could have taken more money. Three hundred bucks is just what she needed to get drugs, and that's all she took."

"I don't blame you at all for what you did," I assured him. "You just cared about Misty and wanted to help her. We all did and we all have regrets."

Once again, I felt a sense that God had placed this person in my path. I had not met David while Misty was working at the Elk's Lodge, yet he was present for an important moment in the final weeks of her life, shedding more light on the fine line she had been trying to walk. She was struggling with the demons but apparently sincere about wanting to break free of them. Fighting alone, without professional help or the support of recovery programs, she just couldn't do it. And with her addiction calling the shots, Misty had again reverted to criminal behavior to maintain her habit.

David professionally steered our meeting back to why we had come. When I told him that I wanted to see my daughter, I saw him glance at Pastor Duane and Buddy with a concerned look.

"Please," I said, "I don't WANT to see my daughter, I NEED to see her." When David and the others kept telling me to trust them, that I simply would not be able to handle the sight of what had happened to my precious daughter, I asked if I could just see her hand. Again, they shook their heads. No, they said, you would not want to see her hands. And the smell is so overwhelming from the hours she lay on the highway in the blistering heat of summer.

"But I have to at least make sure it's really Misty," I said. "The police said the body was unrecognizable so maybe…"

David nodded his head and directed his staff to take photos of Misty's tattoos—one of a phoenix rising and one of Rick's name. When they showed those photos to me, I had all the proof I needed. They clipped a piece of her brown hair for us to take home, and later I lovingly shampooed and dried her hair in the sun, watching the red highlights glimmer as I imagined Misty brushing her hair that always smelled so good when I hugged her.

We finished making arrangements for the cremation. Each of her sons would receive a locket embellished with her fingerprint and filled with a pinch of her ashes. Her siblings and I would receive a necklace with her fingerprint printed on a rectangular charm. We were gifted with a beautiful tapestry blanket weaving in photos from Misty's life and readily agreed to have another version of that tapestry hang in the conference room of the mortuary, a beautiful advertisement for other bereaved family members who might want a similar blanket. I knew that I would love having that blanket in my home, and I could imagine Misty's sons reaching out to see it more closely, to touch it, just as they would want to be touching their mother in the flesh….

Hospital photo of Misty Brooke Musick, whom we lovingly called our little newborn Eskimo baby because of all that dark hair. In my daydreams, as a teen, I visualized my baby girl with blond hair and blue eyes. I was shocked when she was born, until I laughingly reminded myself that her Daddy has dark hair.

April 16, 1981

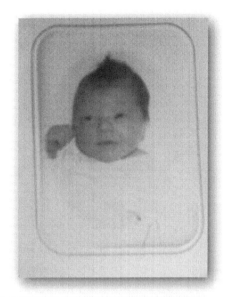

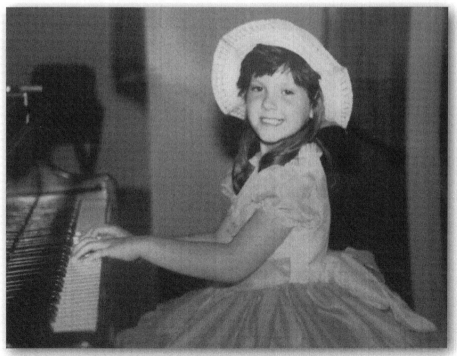

1986 Five year old Misty at her first piano recital.
She is wearing one of the fancy dresses that Grandma purchased for her.

Mother's Day at Mount Hope Assembly of God (above)
Buddy and Misty Father-Daughter banquet (below) unknown date.

(L-R) Back row Brian, Michael, Janelle, Shannon, Misty, Josh
(L-R) Cheryl, Buddy

(Below) Typical Musick family antics

(Left) Mark, at the wedding of Janelle and Travis. October 2011

(Below) Heartbreaking regression- Mug Shot October 2013

Josiah, Misty's youngest Son, would climb onto the shelf below the
dividing glass during visits to his Mother in jail to get as close to
her as possible. Cuddling with an exhausted Misty, this photo was
taken the day after she was released from Yavapai county jail.

(Top) Misty and her Sons-all smiles just days after her release.
(Bottom) One of the last pictures taken of Misty and her siblings

Before her relapse, Misty enjoyed spending time with the horses at the ranch. This photo now hangs on a tapestry at David's Funeral Home.

The horrific scene at I-17 and Dixileta. Misty's twisted and broken body lies under the yellow tarp, Johnny was buckled and sleeping in the front passenger seat and miraculously, the driver, James Washington stood up in the middle of this heap of twisted metal, surviving with a few stitches and bruises. July 27, 2015

(Top) In the gravel beside the wreckage. Detective Waltermire was ready to leave the scene when this piece of evidence was found. He was immediately assigned to the crime scene.

(Bottom) Detective Waltermire's willingness to answer my distressed questions and make himself available to come to our home to help get a clearer picture of the events of July 27, 2015 became a healing balm to this Mother's heart.

Misty's Memorial Cross at I-17 and Dixileta. The two crosses can be seen on the hill before passing the Dixileta bridge going south on the I-17

The two plaques I created to place at the foot of the cross

While visiting Michael and his family in Tennessee, we made an appointment to get matching tattoos in honor of Misty. The design represents the pain of knowing we will never hear Misty play the piano again. It is a dark rose weaving its way through broken piano keys-The Day the Musick Died. March 2016

I suppose some parents in my situation would not care to know any more of the details of the collision that claimed my daughter's life. If your child is gone, did it really matter exactly how it all happened? To me, it did. I needed to have a complete picture of the final moments of Misty's life to hold onto, to help me begin to put it all together, to make sense of it. So I called the detective who happened to be right behind the minivan Misty was riding in. I learned that his name was James Waltermire and that his official position was Detective with the Criminal Investigation Division of the Vehicular Crimes Unit of the Arizona Department of Public Safety. Every question I asked, he was right there to answer it, in as much detail as I wanted to hear.

He told me that he had been traveling in the #2 lane of the three traveling lanes on I-17 when he saw the minivan in the #1 lane drift toward the parked truck-trailer and run over the triangles before smashing into the left rear corner of the truck. He witnessed Misty's body being thrown from the vehicle and onto the roadway. He saw the driver stand up in that mangled minivan, with its roof ripped off all the way to the back. As the detective went on to explain:

I stopped in front of the semi, kicked on my lights and began to set up to block traffic. Then I ran back and saw... Misty, who was obviously deceased. I helped the driver out of the minivan. Soon a sergeant in our unit arrived and we moved further to the side of the road to talk to the driver, who was obviously shaken up.....When the sergeant moved in to speak to the driver further, I took out a blanket to cover Misty. The morning rush hour was continuing to drive by the scene.

Hearing of this simple gesture filled me with gratitude for this kind, thoughtful detective. I knew that he was personally impacted by what he had witnessed. Although he was used to coming upon gruesome scenes of fatal collisions in his professional role, he wasn't at all accustomed to watching the scene unfold live, right before his eyes. "Am I really seeing what I'm seeing?" he asked himself. He also understood that the woman ejected from the minivan was somebody's daughter.

Detective Waltermire thought that he would be leaving the scene within minutes because he only investigated accidents where a crime was involved. Initially, he had not encountered any signs of that. It was entirely possible that the driver had simply fallen asleep. Then he came across the pieces of the broken meth pipe in the road, along with a little blue container that drug users put their dope in. Drugs were involved, which meant a crime. He would remain on the case.

Through further questioning of the driver, whose name was James Washington, more details spilled out. Apparently Misty and her two companions had driven up from Wickenburg in the predawn hours that morning, traveling along the same route we would routinely take to Phoenix: Route 60 east out of town, across the desert on Route 74, and then onto I-17 South for the direct route into the Phoenix area. Why did Misty wind up in a minivan? From what I could determine, she and Johnny had sold the green Honda Civic that they had been driving while living on the lam. The driver said he didn't know Misty and Johnny until recently, when they told him they had traveled to Phoenix in a Greyhound bus. I wondered, but did not know, if the three of them had been involved in some kind of criminal activity the night before the collision.

According to the driver, Misty had actually been at the wheel of the minivan when they started out that morning. He said that she was swerving and struggling to stay awake, so he suggested that he take over either just before or just after they exited Route 74 and turned onto I-17. If Misty had still been driving, would she and her fellow passengers have met with the same fate? We would never know.

The minivan had apparently seen better days. The middle seat had been torn out and a love seat had been inserted to give passengers a place to sit. As the minivan approached the Dixileta Bridge, Johnny was asleep up front beside the driver and Misty was on that love seat until she had stood up and leaned toward the front, supposedly to place her cell phone charger in the cigarette lighter. The driver insisted that he did not remember what happened from there.

So where were Misty and Johnny, along with this driver, headed that morning? What were they up to? I was left only with a handful of clues and the theories of others who may or may not have known something. We heard that Misty and Johnny had recently been sleeping in the backyard of one of their drug dealer friends in the Phoenix area. Maybe they were headed back there. That idea did not disturb me as much as the other evidence gathered at the crash site: a hand gun, ski masks, gloves and stolen credit cards. When I heard about them carrying those supplies, I remembered the day I sat with Misty in Rick's apartment soon after his death when she showed me those poster boards of their next planned "hit" while proudly informing me of a robbery she had already committed. Was my daughter on her way to commit another robbery the day she died? I had to admit that it was very possible.

Lots of terrible things could have happened had the minivan not plowed into that tractor-trailer. Misty could have been involved in some crime in which the gun was used and someone got hurt or killed. She could have linked up with a pimp, agreeing to share her body despite the disgrace and the danger. She could have been a party to major loss and suffering by the people whose IDs had been stolen to meet the needs of the runaway addicts. Perhaps she and Johnny really were going to make some bizarre attempt to flee across the border to Mexico, and if they ever succeeded they could easily have become entangled with Mexican drug lords. With these and other possible scenarios flashing through my tired brain, I imagined receiving a phone call or a knock on the door with other kinds of devastating and heartbreaking news about Misty. Maybe there would have been a whole series of those calls or police visits. The addiction that had latched its evil claws into Misty's flesh was calling the shots, not the person that was Misty trapped inside.

For that reason, many people who knew and loved me gently suggested that perhaps what happened to Misty was in some hard-to-explain way a relief. Misty was gone and nothing would ever change that; nothing could ever wipe away the pain or fill the hole in my heart. But maybe her passing this way at least put an end to the struggle. Misty no longer had to battle her addiction, and we as a family no longer had to live with the fear, the terror and the outlandishness of what was happening and what might happen next. In those early days of grief I wasn't quite ready to define the tragedy that simply, but I could easily understand the thinking of those who embraced that idea.

I was clear about one thing: Misty's memorial service would not dwell on her drug addiction. Everyone there knew about that. We would not hide from the truth and the subject would come up appropriately, but it was much more important to celebrate the real Misty, the woman who melted hearts with her music, cared about others and lit up every room she entered. Misty Brooke Musick Sanchez was far, far more than someone who had engaged in a battle with heroin and other destructive drugs and didn't win.

Keeping in mind Misty's zany sense of humor, we requested that everyone who attended come wearing mismatched socks. From her days growing up with us and on into raising her own three kids, Misty *never* seemed to have an easy time coming up with matching socks to wear. We requested that everyone dress down, casual as Misty would have wanted it—no funeral black or suits and ties. Brian and our friend Jeremy worked for hours on a touching and humorous video of Misty's life from birth to just weeks before her demise.

So there we were back at Mount Hope Assembly of God, where Misty had spent so many wonderful and difficult moments in her life. Pastor Duane officiated the service for the woman he had watched grow up and whom he taught to sing. I remember parts of the eulogy that Misty's friend Hailey delivered; reflecting on the day Misty invited her home for what she called a "Mexican Fiesta." With wild notions of what that would be in her head, Hailey arrived to find only a simple family barbecue with Mark and the boys, all tanned and brown skinned from their Mexican heritage. Misty loved to play practical jokes. "There wasn't anything we didn't do together or think we couldn't do. She was the sister I never had," Hailey said.

Mark spoke affectionately about the girl he met during *For Unto Ya'll*, the music they shared and the good times they had experienced in the past. He delivered a touching message to each of their sons, as I held Brendon and Josiah in my arms while they wept. Brian spoke of his closeness with Misty as her brother, and he also touched upon Misty's battle with drugs. "Misty once told me to imagine the worst fever ever and not having any Tylenol to break it," he explained of his talk with her about what it's like to come down off heroin. "Then imagine your bones breaking over and over and over again, all over your body, and you can't stop it. The only way to stop is to continue using."

Oh, there was one more very important component of Misty's memorial service: music. There *had* to be music.

Even today, more than a year after I lost my daughter, I can hardly sit still long enough to play the DVD of the opening of Misty's memorial. It begins with piano playing—Misty's precious fingers dancing on the keyboard creating a magical sound. Later, in the video montage of her life, there is a lengthy video clip of one of our family Christmas celebrations. We are gathered around the piano, but Misty is not playing this time. She is standing tall and proud and singing: "*Silent Night, Holy Night, all is calm, all is bright...*"

That is how I want to remember my beloved daughter Misty.

CHAPTER 9

— co—

The Wreckage

They say, "Smile and remember the happy times, the good times." Sometimes I do, but do they comprehend what it's really like to lose your child? Do they understand the immense sharpness of the pain when they make that well-intentioned suggestion? The idea of pondering the happy times may sound great, and as I look at these pictures I am able to smile...as my heart is breaking and tears sting my eyes because I do remember her life, her smile, her hugs, her cries in the night, her wet diapers, her fevers, her scraped knees, her fingers on the piano keys, her first steps, the braces on her teeth, her hair, those hazel eyes–all of her–the very things that I miss so very much. I smile, I remember, I hurt, I cry. Maybe they just don't understand... –From a July 2016 posting on the Facebook page "Misty Brooke Musick Sanchez: Addictions–a Painful Journey of Hope."

THERE IS A common saying you hear often from drug addicts who stubbornly resist admitting to their problem and seeking treatment while they go about ruining their lives: "We are only hurting ourselves." Do not believe them! Through all their destructive choices and behavior, addicts cause pain and suffering to everyone who loves them. That anguish follows families like ours all along the trail of horrible acts, lies and manipulation, fear and terror that we get swept up on. The pain and torment never leave, even after the addict's own suffering ceases at the moment of death.

That is why my story does not end, cannot end, with the recounting of Misty's violent death on July 27, 2015. Because when you love someone who is never able to break the chains of addiction, you continue to live that story of the painful impact of addiction with every breath that you take.

I began devoting my time and energy into writing this book in the period around the one-year anniversary of that fatal crash on I-17. I thank God that I have been blessed to experience waves of understanding, healing and grace in my grief, but losing Misty still hurts to the core. A couple of days before the anniversary, I wrote:

"I had a rough morning after driving through the round-about behind a big rig. My eyes focused on the bumper guard, the very thing that is supposed to keep cars from going under the truck. As I drove, I couldn't stop thinking about Johnny and Misty. Who went first? They were milliseconds apart, two young souls dying together on that freeway...."

As hard as I have tried to forget, I still vividly remember that day when the three police officers knocked on our door with news that triggered my blood-curdling scream. I can't forget any of it: the detailed description of the crash provided by the compassionate detective who happened to witness it; my hopelessness on the phone as my youngest son Josh frantically beat the walls upon hearing the news that his big sister was gone; the beautiful but haunting sounds of Misty's piano playing captured in the video shared at her memorial service; the attractive black urn holding her ashes in my kitchen. Nor can I forget all the anguish of those last few years, after the demons had invaded Misty's life and refused to let go.

A year after our loss, I felt called to revisit many of the places and people that had been a part of Misty's painful journey. I also engaged in conversations with others who have been impacted by my daughter's death because I *needed* to keep talking about it. I have also spent quiet times reflecting upon moments and images that have unfolded over the long months since my daughter's passing. In a way, I was surveying the wreckage scene, not out of some morbid obsession to keep re-living what happened but more in the spirit of detectives who comb the site in search of evidence and clues to help them sort out the puzzle. That is what I have been seeking: clues that could help me learn, understand and integrate this tragedy into the lives that all of us who loved Misty must go on living. Perhaps, in sifting through the mental, physical, emotional and spiritual wreckage, I also might gain insights that I could pass along to other addicts and their loved ones. If there is one thing I have learned from this experience, it is that we all have so much to offer one another when we share our pain and the wisdom we may have gained through our suffering.

So, in that spirit, here are some reflections from the aftermath of losing my daughter to drug addiction:

I remember showing Carlos, Brendon and Josiah the blanket with the photo collage of their mother woven into it when they came for a week-long visit. "Would you like to sleep with this tonight?" I asked Josiah, Misty's youngest. When Josiah nodded, I asked him if he wanted to see his mom's urn. I explained that the urn held her ashes and also her clothes and the shoes she was wearing that day. As he cradled the urn in his arms, his big brown eyes appeared to expand. "Would you like to keep the urn with you during the night?" I asked. Soon he and his big brother Carlos were carefully selecting just the right spot for the urn on the end table in the "beach" room of our home, and then they rearranged the futon and bedding so Josiah could be as close as possible to his mother's ashes while he slept. I gathered all three boys around the blanket for a photo, and I still cry whenever I look at it....

I remember listening to Lisa when she came to our house to tearfully confess how she had concealed Misty and Johnny's presence in her home from us that night not long before the crash. "I should have told you she was there. I should have called you as soon as Misty and Johnny showed up at my door," Lisa said. As she sobbed, I locked her in a firm embrace. "We forgive you, Lisa," I said softly. "We forgive you."

I had decided that when I came face to face with those involved in the final days of Misty's life, I was not going to blame anyone—not Lisa, not the driver of the minivan, not Johnny, not her slow-moving PO, no one. As a Christian, I always seek to find room in my heart to forgive. And as the mother of a drug addict, I knew that addiction turns everything upside down and then swirls it up into a massive ball of confusion. We were all doing the best we could. No one deserved blame or malice. Lisa was an addict herself, trapped in the same dark, secretive world that Misty was living in, where you don't tell others the truth about what you're doing or where you're doing it. Sometimes sharing that information can even be dangerous. My only wish for Lisa was that, after getting sent back to prison, she could embrace recovery in a way that Misty never could….

I remember spending the holidays alone with Buddy. On Thanksgiving, we solemnly ate dinner at a buffet by ourselves, something we had never done on that family holiday. We sat quietly as we simply looked each other in the eyes and said a prayer—so tearful, so painful—but we were together. In my Facebook post that night I wrote:

"We are thankful because we know that God was there even on that day of the accident, and is here with us, for the rest of our beautiful family, and for our supportive church families and friends who care for us, and for each person who takes the time to read and like this Facebook page so others may receive support and encouragement, and for those who reach out to offer support to me and my family, and for God's protection over our marriage that the two of us as Husband and Wife and best friends can walk and sometimes stumble through this fire together. We are thankful

for our grown children all handling their sister's death differently and in particular for Brian who unknowingly joined forces against the addiction enemy by simply posting his heart on Facebook. We give thanks in our quiet conversations and prayers, not for pity but simply as another stage in our journey of grief, the loss of our grown child, our first-born, whom we nurtured, fed, changed, bought Christmas presents for, held, hugged, reprimanded, celebrated birthdays, loved and worried over. For everyone reading this post, Happy Thanksgiving! Embrace your loved ones; hold them close enough to feel their hearts beating with life and love."

We also chose to keep Christmas simple and quiet. We didn't buy presents for anyone except our grandchildren and teenage son Josh. We didn't even decorate the house. I didn't want to be around anyone, not even my own family. There would be no singing of *Silent Night*. However, there was one thing I did want to do...something for Misty.

So a week or two before Christmas, we drove up to I-17 near the Dixileta Bridge to visit the memorial cross that we had erected for our daughter on the hillside overlooking the site of the crash that ended her life. The idea for a cross originated with one of Johnny's co-workers in the Yavapai County jail kitchen. After she put up a memorial cross for Johnny, we decided to put one up for Misty beside it. I had already visited the scene of the crash, just because I had to see it, and to gather remnants to take home. Leaving a permanent mark there to honor Misty's memory and to warn drivers to be careful made perfect sense.

The wooden cross has a rock foundation built over a cement block. Her age and date of her passing is marked at the top, with the words "Misty Musick Sanchez: Beloved Mother, Sister, Daughter and Wife" running across the middle. On the lower part of the cross we added her favorite Bible scripture, Jeremiah 29:11 (*"For I know the plans I have for you," declares the Lord, "plans to prosper you and not to harm you, plans to give you hope and a future.")* In the rocks below are two ceramic discs, one teal and one red, that proclaim: "Misty, I witnessed your first breath. Miss you, Mom" and "Daughter Misty, it was here you took your last breath 7-27-15."

Some callous individual knocked the crosses down one day, stealing the solar lights that illuminated them at night. Buddy drove to the site and secured them back to their original positions. Now, for Christmas, Buddy picked out a perfect little white tree, investing the kind of time and careful attention in his selection that Misty and her siblings would devote to finding our family tree every Christmas so long ago. We wrapped Misty's cross in red garland and green bulbs. It felt good to simply stand there and look, and remember....

I remember the visit we had at home with Detective James Waltermire, the witness to Misty's accident. After patiently answering our questions over the phone, he volunteered to take time out of his busy schedule to come to our house to show us the formal accident report and allow us to view any photos that we chose to see. My daughter Shannon and my Daughter-in-law Heather were brave enough to look at the pictures of Misty's body on the pavement of I-17, and they confirmed that what I was told at the funeral home was correct: I would NOT want to see it. From what I understand, her face hit the pavement and she lay face down. However, her body was twisted so that her bottom half was face up. I did choose to look at one smaller photo inserted into a section of the report, showing only Misty's hand. As soon as I glimpsed that photo, I had to turn away. Those delicate fingers that played such beautiful music on the piano were twisted and turned so that they pointed in opposite directions. It was then that I understood why no one allowed me to get a glimpse of her.

Detective Jim was so patient and considerate in the way he responded to my questions and allowed me to decide what to examine and what to keep to the side. The more time he spent with us, the more he felt like part of our family. He was even willing to share his personal background: he was born in Africa as the son of missionaries, his wife was a former addictions counselor, and he had two young daughters of his own. He understood what we were experiencing and cared about us as people, not just names on some official report about one more drug-related fatality. "Visiting with you brings back the humanness for me," he said. "When you see this sort of thing with addicts day in and day out, you can get hardened to it. Now I remember that there is always a family that loves and cares for that person." Again, I felt deep gratitude for God placing Jim at that scene, and now bringing him into our lives and our hearts....

I remember learning more chilling details about the accident via contact with the driver of the tractor-trailer and his family. Apparently, this driver, whom I will call Phil, had been standing outside near the rear of his truck only minutes before the minivan came barreling into the breakdown lane. Then a voice, which could only have been God, told him to get back in his cab and stay there. Had he remained outside, he would have become an innocent victim of a crash caused by three people using drugs. I will keep other details that Phil shared in confidence, except to say that I was delighted to learn that he also was a devout Christian and that from the first moments after the minivan struck his truck, he displayed genuine caring and compassion toward our family and to the memory of Misty....

I remember reaching out to Johnny's family to offer our prayers and support. Some people may wonder why I wouldn't be furious at this young man, a meth dealer, who showed up at our doorstep and, seemingly whisked our daughter back to a life of drugs, danger and darkness. But I knew Johnny—I had glimpsed his heart and could separate the person from the addict. I also understood that the choices Misty made were hers alone. I had seen a photo of Johnny with his younger brother. I grieved for Johnny's family....

I remember how David was not the only person at the funeral home touched by Misty's death. One of his staff members, Phoebe, had known Misty well when they were kids. "We were close friends during elementary school and went to high school together," Phoebe told me during one of our stops at David's Desert Chapel. "She was always the leader of our group—doing gymnastics, turning cartwheels, hanging upside down on the monkey bars, making up goofy plays. We always believed she was going to do big things in life. I hadn't seen her since she was nineteen, and when she showed up here, well, I took it pretty hard. I have a little girl and when I went home after work that night I cried to her. When she asked me why I was crying, I told her all about Misty…."

I vividly remember suffering through another family tragedy when my daughter Janelle lost her baby during childbirth, only five months after Misty died. His name is Lincoln, and I was crushed that this devastating loss had to fall on the shoulders of the daughter who had the strongest and most natural maternal instinct. I was there to witness what happened, along with Janelle's loving husband Travis, and in the empty and painful days that followed I was left to wonder why our family had to endure a second sudden death in the same year. There are mysteries for which we will never hold answers….

As I've carried the heartache of the past several months, it has been cathartic and sometimes healing to share my emotions on the Facebook page that I created for Misty's memory and for the cause of easing the suffering of addiction. Just weeks before what would have been Misty's thirty-fifth birthday in April 2016, I wrote this to my daughter:

Dear Misty,

Today I will get a tattoo in your memory. It will not be angels, clouds, bright flowers, butterflies, crosses or any other typical memorial symbols. It will be a reminder of what could have been, of what was supposed to be before alcohol, before Meth, before Heroin and a reminder of our devastating loss, a loss I see in the eyes of your Daddy, the same painful gaze I see in my own eyes when I look into the mirror. My tattoo will be a dark reminder to others to stay away from the toxins that lead to addiction. Some will take note, others like you, unfortunately, will throw it all away for the demons that flood veins, arteries, stomachs, brains and souls.

This morning I opened my Bible to Mark 14:38, a warning from Jesus himself: "watch and pray so that you will not fall into temptation. The spirit is willing, but the body is weak." You cheated death so often—what a stupid thing you three did that last day! I'm so thankful you guys didn't kill or injure anyone else. I miss you, Misty, not the addict but my intelligent, beautiful, talented, fun daughter. I hurt, your Dad hurts, your Siblings hurt. I feel sad, angry, depressed, and now and then I can forget, and feel joyful.

That tattoo on my upper arm depicts broken piano keys with a darkened rose intertwined; representing what was and is no more. When I look at it today, I sometimes think of the words that Misty once shared with me: "Mom, I wish I had never put that needle in my arm, because all it took was that one time and that was it." I am always willing to explain my tattoo to anyone who is curious—you never know when it may stop someone from using drugs.

My suffering is only part of the anguish that our whole family has shared. I carry a vivid snapshot image in my mind of the way that my five remaining children came together, sobbing and huddled in a long embrace during Misty's memorial service. As time has gone on, they have grieved Misty's death in their own way.

Shannon still remembers her sister asking for her urine to pass a drug test and buying a detox solution at a smoke shop to get past another test. "Johnny and Misty stayed with us overnight; we even let them sleep in our bed," she recalls. "In the morning I would come into the bedroom expecting to see the worst: either they'd be using or they had OD'd." When Shannon read her brother Brian's Facebook post expressing his anger over Misty's death, she found herself in 100 percent agreement. "Misty had made the decision to leave our family a long time ago," she sighs. "She was selfish and using us.

Her death was so sad but it was also just frustrating. She broke our hearts."

Janelle told me that she had a few dreams of Misty, in her old self, laughing and hugging and doing things for others. Otherwise, she has not felt much lingering closeness. Like Shannon, she experienced Misty leaving long before those final months. She was never optimistic that Misty could climb the ladder of recovery. Even when she went out of her way to spend time with Misty after her release from jail, Janelle just didn't sense a real commitment on her sister's part to do the work needed to get clean. Today, she worries about Misty's three boys, whom she has come to love dearly. "I know them, and I trust that that they will get through this and grow into really good men," she says.

Josh, still a teenager when this all happened, has continued to take it very hard. Several months after Misty's death, he went on Facebook to share his feelings:

"Misty, I still try so hard every day to find the words to explain how much you mean to me. When you first went to the needle, my pain was unexplainable. I was pissed off, punching the walls in my room, screaming into a pillow, chain-smoking cigarettes until my lungs hurt. You went to jail after a car accident and I really had hoped that it would help you get clean and change you. Little did I know that your life would be taken less than a year after you got out. My mind still replays the day that Mom told me you passed. All the screaming, all the curse words. Nearly blacked out running into the walls of the house while Brent and Shannon sat there speechless until she finally grabbed me and held me while I screamed into her shoulder. I wish my mind would stop replaying that moment, but it just won't. I wish things were different. You had everything. You were my oldest sister. You were supposed to be my role model. My second mom. Why the f--- did you have to turn to drugs, Sister? My heart is torn

and I don't think it will ever heal. Some days I find it hard to believe that everything happens for a reason because all I wanted was for you to stay clean. I miss your smile. I miss your hugs. I miss hearing you call me Baby Brother. I love you, big sister. Forever and always."

As for Brian, a year after writing "I am far beyond angry" over Misty's destructive choice to keep going back to drugs rather than embracing a healthy life, he told me "I'm still really mad about it." He tries not to think about his sister, but her memory still pops into his head sometimes. Two days before the one-year anniversary of the crash, he went back to Facebook and spoke to Misty directly:

> "I miss harmonizing with you, Misty. Why couldn't you just embrace The Music and sing for me? So beautiful and dark, the music that we could have created. You were my Angel of Music..."

During a visit with Brian and Heather at their home, my son made it clear that he had a lot more to say about what had happened:

"Misty didn't have to go through what a lot of addicts go through. Many of them are alone, with no love and support from family. But when Misty got out of jail, she had a place to stay, she had food and clothes, she had someone in town offer her a job; she had other family close by. I gave her a car. And still, even after receiving all those things that other addicts never have, she fell right back into using drugs. The whole ordeal was just so maddening. I'm a logical, rational person and this entire ordeal is just madness, insanity, and chaos. There is no way to put rational thought to it."

Heather shared her husband's frustration. "I was angry because Misty through her actions was hurting her parents, and she just did not care. She wanted to do what she wanted to do and it didn't matter to her if she hurt Mom or Dad," she told me. "I wanted to shake her and say, 'You have a wonderful family that's showing you that they're there to support you, to help you get out of this mess. And you're turning your back on them.' I have known a lot of drug addicts and most of them don't have a family there to say, 'We still love you, let's get help.' I really think the families of drug addicts suffer more than the addicts themselves. We're not the ones taking the drugs and suffering those physical effects but we are there watching them every step and doing everything we can to help them, even when they don't want the help. It's so hard."

Heather speaks from experience because addiction has run rampant through her own family. Her father still struggles with addiction, and her sister, who happened to be a nurse as Misty was, was found in a gutter after an overdose. Fortunately, she survived. Heather's nephew has also been battling drugs, but the good news there is that Misty's death woke him up and he has made it a whole year without relapsing. Maybe that's one life that Misty can be a part of saving.

Brian takes issue with those who dare to suggest that people like Misty have no choice other than to keep using drugs because they're addicted. "You mean to say it wasn't my sister's choice to use again after being clean for a year and a half?" he says. "If that's the case, then a serial killer cannot help but kill people since that is their demon. An addict will always battle the demon of drugs. Misty described to me how hard that is physically. I understand that. And I understand that they may slip up from time to time. But when a person completely gives up the battle, that is a choice. And Misty, even with all the help and support available to her, chose to give up."

As Brian spoke those words, I remembered that Shannon had shared similar feelings about Misty and the opportunities she had. "I always believe that even in your deepest, darkest moment, you have a choice," Shannon reflected. "Even in those final days when she was running, Misty still had that little voice telling her, 'No, don't do this.' But she ignored that voice, and she just kept going."

Heather and Brian are committed to educating their own two children about addiction. As parents, they are choosing not to hide the reality of what really happened to their Aunt Misty. That's one of the many lessons we all continue to learn about this painful journey: you can't hide from what's happening with an addict, and you can't hide from the devastating effects on everyone involved.

I was reminded of that lesson again when I arrived for a catch-up visit with Roy Thomas at Bridges Network, the treatment center that Misty agreed to enter but then chose to leave—long before she had given herself any real opportunity to build and maintain a recovery program. As I walked along the corridor outside Roy's office, my eyes went straight to that photo collage he displays on the wall as a memorial for all those addicts who didn't make it. Misty's photo now has its place, in the lower left side of the lineup.

"Some days I think about taking down that collage and sticking it in the closet so I wouldn't have to see it or think about it," Roy says softly. "But it's part of our reality. It's always sad when someone that we treat in our program doesn't make it. But I remember something my dad told me when he worked at Remuda Ranch in Wickenburg. A young woman on his caseload killed herself soon after she left treatment. My dad was pouring out all his feelings about this tragedy and suddenly he said, 'You know, I don't need this crap anymore. I'm getting out of this work.' But he spent some time thinking about it and finally he got to the point where he said, 'You know, if I quit, the dragon wins.' Thank God there are many, many addicts who come to treatment that are saved. We see people change here, their lives transformed. I firmly believe that recovery is possible for everybody. There's no reason Misty could not have…nobody is so sick that they can't get well. But some won't."

Roy's heart goes out to the families of all those men and women whose faces are featured on that collage. He has stood by our family throughout this experience, and he has become one of my biggest supporters in my mission to try to save the lives of addicts through my Facebook page and now through this book. He made me smile when he told me that he could imagine Misty's voice saying "Go, Mom!"

"I am a recovering addict, but I didn't really understand the pain that I caused my family until I started talking to all the other families in my program," Roy explains. "It's painful to have a family member struggle with addiction, but the addict needs that support from family to have the best chance at recovery. We have a very strong and active family program here at our center because I'm convinced that if we get the addict on the road to recovery but then send them back to the same toxic living situation, they are almost doomed to relapse. We have to make an impact on the family so that when the addict goes home, he or she can build on what they have done here."

And yet, as Roy understands, family members must take on the challenge of walking a fine line. Yes, they need to be present in the life of the addict and offer their love, support, encouragement and compassion. They also need to somehow recognize when they may be getting in the way.

"When I look back at the eight times I made an attempt at recovery and failed, I remember that one of the main things that was different in my last episode of treatment was a change in what my father did," Roy notes. "My life would get in trouble because of my addiction, and I'd call my father and say, 'Dad, I need help.' And he'd jump on a plane, wherever I was, and walk me through detox. He did it over and over and over again. This last time, I was staying in St. Louis. When Dad had visited me there earlier, he had a chance to meet my sponsor. He had gone back home to Arizona when I relapsed again. 'Dad, I need help,' I said, as I always did. So he jumped on the first plane to St. Louis and arranged to meet my sponsor at the airport. When they met, my sponsor said, 'Do you really want to help your son? Then go home.' Without even coming to my hotel to say hello, my dad turned around and flew home. And that was the last time I ever used drugs."

Misty didn't commit to the program at Bridges long enough for Buddy and I, and all our family, to really sink into the learning process of helping the addict without getting in the way, without enabling. Certainly family members need to do whatever is possible to help their loved one get treatment and stand with that individual every step of the way. Yes, they can offer them a helping hand until they get their feet on the ground during that period when recovery is fragile, as we tried to do with Misty after she got out of jail. But then you have to pay attention to when your impulse to help goes too far. For example, the addict you love tells you they have run out of money—whether from using again or acting in some other irresponsible way—and need you to pay for their cell phone. Well, you want them to have a phone so they can call you, but if you pay for that phone you may be hurting them. How? Because addicts need to suffer the consequences of their behavior before they'll ask for help.

What we family members need to understand is that addicts do not change unless they really want to change. Somehow or other, you need to give them the opportunity to tap that desire to change and finally make those choices that you so desperately hope they will make. It's a baffling, frustrating dance, and when the addict that you love never turns the corner, never accesses that deep wanting to live, you can't help asking yourself all sorts of questions about what you did or didn't do. You find yourself playing out scenarios, and they all seem to begin with the same two words:

If only.

Even Roy carries his "if only" regarding Misty, and he's an experienced professional in drug treatment with his own personal background as an addict in recovery. "If only we could have gotten Misty into a lockdown unit," he said. Yet Roy knew that Misty was determined to go off and do what she thought she had to do after Rick's death, even though she was demonstrating what some addiction experts call "stinkin' thinkin'."

David at the funeral home heard the echoes of "if only" when he remembered his response to finding out that Misty had stolen money from the Elk's Lodge. "If only I had turned her in," he would say. Yet even if he had reported her, Misty might have run away before the police closed in on her, and even if she had gone back to jail she may have just followed the same path she chose after getting out of jail the first time. No one knows. Anyway, in his heart David believed he was helping Misty and he trusted that she would do what she promised. She had become very good at making people trust her.

Lisa was certainly toting a hefty "if only" when she came to visit us. When Buddy was on the phone trying to find Misty and Misty was right there with her, Lisa believes that *if only* she had told Buddy that Misty was there, then we would have been able to track her down and get her to her probation officer and most likely to jail. Is that what would have happened? Who knows? Lisa, too, thought she was helping her good friend Misty, whom she knew not only from jail but also in their volunteer work together at the Elk's Lodge where Lisa's community service hours were fulfilled by leading bingo games. That was where Misty had introduced Lisa to meth, by the way. She had been manipulated by Misty, too, and she was confused.

I'm not sure, but it's possible that Misty's sisters may have had their own "if only" tapes playing from the very first days when they knew that she had a drinking problem, or when they learned from Misty that she had first used drugs not while in her toxic relationship with Rick but way back in her unhealthy first marriage to Brad when she was barely an adult. If they had come to me and Buddy with their concerns, might we all have acted sooner to try to get Misty help? Could we have gotten through that exterior wall she put up, her denial that she had a problem, if we had begun chipping away much earlier and kept pounding and pounding at it through the years?

I certainly have had my "if only" moments. Sometimes I wonder if we could have attempted a family intervention. I understand the potential value of bringing everyone together with the addict under one roof and, one by one, truthfully explaining in detail how the addict's behavior was negatively impacting them, and then emphasizing their love and concern for the addict along with a firm request to get help, which ideally would be backed up by a concrete plan ready to implement. Could the Musicks have waged a successful family intervention with Misty? My first thought is that it would not have mattered if we tried because Misty had communicated to us consistently that:

1) She did not believe in drug treatment; and
2) She resented anyone in her family suggesting that she must get treatment in order for them to still love her. But perhaps we were too quick to back down. Maybe there would have been strength in numbers. Maybe we could have knocked that wall down. Maybe....

That possibility lingers as one of my many "if only" storylines. *If only* I had turned Misty and Johnny in as soon as I saw the signs of them using meth and heroin. *If only* I had never allowed Johnny to live in our house in the first place, or at least if I only allowed that to happen with a firm contract from the very beginning rather than far down the road of unhealthy behavior. *If only* I had made different parenting choices with Misty when she was growing up, then maybe she would not have been wounded in ways that could have contributed to her addiction, along with the contributions from her genes and everything else, of course.

Fortunately, I have learned of the critical need to let go of all those "if only" messages rattling around my brain. It all comes back to this: we all did our best with what we knew at the time. We didn't have a manual for how to deal with an addict in our family. No one has an absolute, fool-proof guide on what to do and what not to do with addiction. At times we sought counsel from others that should know, and often their answers conflicted with one another or showed clear signs that the generalities they referred to did not take into consideration the individual person that Misty was. They're not the mother.

I saw a therapist for much of my first year of living without Misty, and I am grateful for the guidance I received. First, I came to recognize more clearly how strong I was as a person, just for persevering after the horrendous childhood that I suffered. I am strong enough to endure after Misty, too. Second, I really understood the importance of not blaming. I may sometimes hear my voice of blame, but I am quick to shut it off. I am not going to blame Cheryl, and I am not going to blame anyone else. That includes James Washington, the man who happened to be at the wheel of the minivan when it slammed into the tractor-trailer and ended my daughter's life.

People told me I should have wanted to scream at that driver, that I should tell him to go to hell. Well, I have to admit that I was a bit surprised myself that I didn't feel angry at this man. Perhaps it was the love of Christ in me that allowed me to open my heart and forgive him. So when I had the opportunity to speak at the sentencing hearing for Mr. Washington in our state Superior Court, I made sure that he knew that I did not blame him for what happened. Of course I had other things I wanted to tell him too:

"The minute we saw your picture on the news, we were not angry with you because I know that you're an addict and you're somebody's child, and for that we forgive you. We're not celebrating that you're going to prison but I'm angry that you guys were in Wickenburg and we were looking for our daughter and she was right there partying with people. I don't even know who they were, and now she's gone. I want you to know the Misty you didn't know. Misty was full of life. Misty was a pianist. She was a singer. She loved the Lord. She brightened the room wherever she went. She was a bright star in our family and we miss her...

Just understand that we don't hate you. And what we want for you, James Washington, is for you to turn your life around. You have a five-year-old son. I don't have my daughter anymore. I have my other children. But he deserves a father, and you can't have both. You can't have your drugs and also a son. And so we wish for you to use that time in prison to work the programs to turn your life around, and maybe find Jesus—I have to say that as a Christian—and to make something good of your life, to be clean and sober. That's all we wish. We don't want money. We don't want anything. We can't have our daughter back. Our thoughts and prayers are going to be with you."

As far as I could tell, not a single family member showed up in the courtroom to support James that day. I felt sad for this precious lost soul. At a later hearing on his case, he wept as he said to Buddy and I, "I am so sorry. Thank you for not hating me."

Through a plea agreement, James received a twelve-year sentence. For those twelve years, and the rest of his life, he will have to live with the reality that his actions, using drugs and driving, caused the deaths of two people. At least Misty was spared his fate, which could have been hers if she had remained at the wheel of that minivan on that July morning.

As a Christian, I wonder about Misty's fate after she was thrown out of that minivan into the black pavement of the interstate. I was thinking about that after a recent visit with Pastor Duane. I no longer attend Mount Hope Assembly of God. As I mentioned before, things happen in churches among people that you love and you must move on. I now attend services at "The Place," a non denomination Christian church in town. However, I still consider Pastor Duane a friend, or more like a brother; someone who has known our family for most of the thirty years we have lived in Arizona. He carries his own special memories of Misty.

"I still remember how Misty taught my daughter Carissa how to test spaghetti: throw it on the wall and see if it sticks," he says with a smile. "All those experiences that any loved one goes through over death, I've been in it too—denial, anger, all of it. Misty was like a daughter to me. She knew I loved her. I know the loss has been so hard on you and Buddy. Parents always ask, 'Am I enabling or am I helping?' We all have our regrets, wondering whether there was something else we could have done. But what we need to understand is that Misty wasn't in her right mind. Drugs change your thinking."

Pastor Duane often ministers to young people struggling with addiction. He understands the demons and the battle. While he was officiating Misty's Celebration of Life, he could look out at the attendees and identify kids that he knew were still using drugs. He took a moment to speak to them: "Get help. We're here." We all hoped that some precious young souls would listen to his words.

Pastor Duane said something else that stuck with me after our visit: "God is a just and fair God. He knows when someone is enslaved. And only God knows that person's heart."

With those words echoing in my mind, I allowed myself to consider a question that I am reluctant to even ask myself: Could Misty have gone to heaven?

I remember when my father died during that Fourth of July celebration in our backyard in California when six-year-old Misty asked me if Grandpa was in heaven, and I answered, "Yes, Grandpa is in Heaven." However, as adults our Christian teachings remind us that it's not as simple as that. The Bible says that you can recognize people by their fruits, and we can't argue with the reality that Misty had some pretty rotten fruit. I mean, can any addict really go to heaven? But if you were to look upon her branches, and see what I saw—that person leading yoga, worship and song while trying to help others in jail where she thrived although she hated it, the person who opened the Bible at home while wrestling with the return of her demons, the person who believed she had to sacrifice her own recovery to take care of a man she loved—they would see something more than the bad fruit of horrible choices and hurtful, destructive behavior.

We all yearn to go to Heaven. I hope that my love for Christ will get me there. I know that I have been born again, and everything that Jesus teaches means so much to me. When I get to Heaven, oh how I would love to walk through the gates and find Misty there! Free. Free of her demons. Near the end she was so sick. God knew that. He knew Misty better than I did. *Only God knows the heart.*

Misty loved to worship when she was healthy. When I think of her today, I want to imagine her as carefree, liberated from everything that had been plaguing her mind. Healed, finally healed, no injuries to her body, youthful and beautiful in a pure way. She wasn't pure when she died, she was badly beaten and…soiled I guess is how I would put it.

I would like to believe that she is fresh now and dancing with Destiny Rose, the baby I lost between Janelle and Shannon, and baby Lincoln who lost his life at birth. I want to imagine her singing *Amazing Grace* for Jesus in that voice that melts like butter.

That is the image I want so badly to cling to, but I am torn. It's difficult to visualize the Lord saying to Misty, "Well done, my good and faithful servant. Enter into the gates of heaven." I mean, there was a gun in that minivan and a mask and fake IDs stolen from other people. Those words do not fit. Instead, perhaps I could imagine Him saying, "I saw your heart, Misty. I saw you struggle. You don't have to struggle now. I love you, daughter. Welcome home."

I can't say that this beautiful scene is crystal clear and ever-present in my mind. It fades in, it fades out. But I won't let it go. During this time of surveying the wreckage from the devastating loss of my precious daughter, it's something that I must hold onto.

CHAPTER 10

—— ❦ ——

A Light in the Darkness

THE YOUNG MALE waiter at the Lone Spur Café across from the Yavapai County Courthouse in the center of Prescott approached our table cautiously. While enjoying lunch with a friend in the Western-themed restaurant with real cowhides hanging on the walls and cowboy boots with spurs mounted above our booth, I was discussing the story of Misty and her many appearances at that courthouse for her drug-related offenses.

"Excuse me," the waiter began. "I don't mean to eavesdrop but I couldn't help over-hearing you. I just wondered...are you in a program?"

"No, but my daughter Misty was a heroin and meth addict," I explained patiently. "We tried to get her in treatment but she didn't make it. She died a year ago."

"Oh, I'm so sorry for you loss," he said.

"Are you in a recovery program?" I asked.

"Yes, I came to a treatment center here in Prescott from Wisconsin and decided to stay so I could focus on my recovery here. I've been clean for a year now."

"Congratulations! I'm so happy for you. Keep with it. You have your whole life ahead of you."

A wide smile swept across his face when I shook his hand. He told me his name was Adam. Looking at this proud and sincere young man, I felt that once again God had placed someone important in my path.

"Misty, that could have been you," I said to myself as I walked out of the restaurant. "You could have done it. You could have followed a recovery program and rebuilt your life like this young man is doing today."

Surprisingly, that thought didn't send waves of sadness and grief washing over me. Instead, I felt tingles—like a ripple of hope. Here before me was a symbol, a heart-stirring reminder that although my daughter lost her battle with drugs, other women and men can still come out on the winning side. There was hope for all the addicts who suffer, and for their families and loved ones who suffer with them. Something good was still possible.

That is the belief that drives me to keep going forward with my mission today. Misty is gone, but there are thousands of people like Adam out there who still have a chance. By continuing to tell our story, I want to be a part of helping them seize the gift extended to them.

For Misty, true recovery would have meant overcoming her resistance to even entering a treatment center, then committing to stay with a program for several months, and after that progressing to a step-down or transitional program where she could work on her core issues, reconnect with her children and find out who the real Misty actually was. She could not embrace that opportunity, as hard as I tried and as often as I prayed for that to happen, but I'm sure there are others who can summon the strength and faith to grab hold of the lifeline and not let go.

Sabrina is one addict who has seized the chance given to her. I met her during a potluck gathering at The Place Church. She recently moved back to Wickenburg after residing in the tiny mountaintop town of Yarnell. This is the area along our route to Prescott that suffered a major fire that claimed the lives of nineteen firefighters, the Prescott Fire Department's Granite Mountain Hotshots not many years ago. There is now a tribute to these 19 brave men on the side of Yarnell hill, a steep climb and walking tour of the area where the fire overtook them. Sabrina told me that she grew up around drugs in her home and fell into that lifestyle herself. She almost lost her life once but now she was off drugs and determined to stay clean. "I just don't want to lose my children," she said. I told her all about Misty, and my mission, and I invited her to breakfast the next time she came through Wickenburg. It turned out that her sister once hung out at our house as a child. Sabrina and I stay in close contact. Perhaps she sees me as someone safe to talk to, someone who understands and won't judge, and I'm doing my best to remain part of her sustaining force to stay on the right path.

I'm in touch with many others determined to win the battle against the demons. Amber has been following our story on Facebook since Brian's angry post just after Misty died. When Amber read that post, she crushed her meth pipe. I'm thrilled to report that she's still clean and sober, and she has helped convince another struggling addict to launch a recovery program. Amber even provides me encouragement when I share my vulnerable feelings on Facebook. "You were a good mom, and Misty knew you loved her," she reassured me.

A few months ago I received a Facebook message from a mother seeking advice on how to deal with her daughter, a young addict living on the streets. The addict was asking her mom for money to support her lifestyle. "Whatever you do, don't give her money," I responded. "Tell her you will help get her into treatment, but that's all." Weeks later she shared the joyous news that her daughter was in recovery. "Thank you, thank you, thank you!" she wrote. "Keep up your Facebook page. It really is helping people."

A long-time family friend who has lived through her son's ups and downs with addiction, recovery and relapse expressed her appreciation for what I was doing. "We can't beat it if we can't talk about it, and most people are afraid to admit that it's their kid doing drugs. What you're doing is helping parents wake up, pull together and try to make a positive change," she said.

These signs of hope excite me whenever or wherever they show up. During my last visit with Roy Thomas at Bridges Network, he shared a story of parents who had lost two children to addiction. A few years after drugs claimed their daughter's life; their son completed a treatment program at Bridges and then kept clean and sober for nine months. Unfortunately, on the day he relapsed, he OD'd. "Now those parents are paying for somebody else to be here, an addict who lacked the resources to pay for treatment," Roy explained. "They're giving back and supporting life."

Roy has a hot seat on the dramatic rise of heroin addiction and other drug and alcohol abuse sweeping our country. In just four years, Bridges has expanded from a 3,000 square feet facility to a bustling enterprise with 100 employees assisting addicts in a treatment center almost seven times larger than what he started.

"I have seen statistics that estimate that there are twenty million addicts out there, and only three million are attempting to get treatment," he said. "Of those three million, only a third of them are successful in finding a treatment center."

We need more treatment centers and more resources for addicts who can't afford the high cost of residential alcohol and drug treatment programs. And we especially need more and more support and encouragement for addicts to reach out and accept the help that's out there for them.

So much needs to change for addicts like Misty to have a chance. Addiction needs to be understood as a physical, moral, emotional and spiritual problem—and a problem that extends to the criminal justice system. Roy agrees with me that addicts who commit a crime while suffering from addiction *must* have a mandated drug treatment program as part of any appropriate sentence or penalty.

"Our prisons are full of addicts, and it doesn't have to be that way," Roy suggests. "Since we now know that addiction is a disease, it should be regarded in a way similar to how we treat something like cancer. We would never shame or punish a person who was treated for cancer and then had the unfortunate occurrence of a relapse. We care for that person. Well, I don't think we should shame or punish a person who relapses in their addiction either. Certainly if they commit a serious crime they should pay for that, but I've seen many addicts who committed horrendous crimes that got clean and sober and never did anything like that again. If we provide treatment for them, in addition to any necessary sentence, they will have a much better chance at gaining sobriety. That would also cut down the number of crimes and the demand on our jails. It's a win-win."

Roy didn't have to convince me. Listening to him reminded me of all those letters my family and I sent to the judge in Misty's case, begging for the court to require rehab treatment for her addiction along with sentencing her to time in jail. Our pleas were not heard. I also remember how the community service requirement for Misty resulted in a position in the Elk's Lodge as a bartender serving alcohol when she should have simply been washing dishes. Despite the challenges of finding any community service options in a small community like Wickenburg, don't try to tell my son Brian that this legally approved arrangement in which Misty was spending hours pouring alcohol made any sense.

I believe that all of us who have witnessed or experienced the damage and destruction caused by addiction are called upon to become stronger and more passionate advocates for greater awareness, understanding and resources for those hooked on alcohol and drugs. We also can embrace the opportunity to share what we have learned in our individual battles with the demons. Even for those like my family whose loved ones lost their battle, we are left with teachings that we can pass along to help others who still have a chance.

I am deeply grateful for what I have learned about addicts and addiction, and the emotional roller-coaster that families often ride. These are really life lessons. As I mentioned earlier, I find that I'm far less judgmental toward other people than I was when raising Misty and her siblings. I recognize that addiction can strike even good people and the best of families, and I understand that no matter what the life of an addict and the families around them may look like from the outside, from the inside they are all regular people trying to do the best they can in what may seem like a hopeless situation. I've learned to accept and love the addict—the person caught in the disease—while hating the addiction. This perspective has helped me to open doors of communication with addicts and their families, and I've tried to bring this non-judgmental attitude into other areas of my life.

In my work with women and men suffering from eating disorders, I find that I'm naturally more empathetic and compassionate toward my patients and their families today. When I am assisting patients in our equine-assisted therapy program, or our ropes course, or other group and individual guidance, I am much better able to understand and relate to their pain, their fears and their frustration. After everything I have gone through with Misty, I am especially understanding of how hard it is for family members to stand with the addict they love in the midst of the daily challenges and torment.

I know first-hand the anguish that comes with this struggle, both for addicts and their loved ones. I also believe that all addicts and families live with a choice. As I tell my groups in our treatment center, you can at any point choose to be either a victim or a victor. You can summon your armor and fight the enemy, or you can give up. For my-self, and for any parent or family member who lost someone to addiction, the choice to remain a victim can feel like a fiercely strong pull. It can define you, and leave you beaten and isolated. My intention is to live more in the spirit of the victor, with the ferocity needed to keep speaking the truth about my daughter while hoping that my words can be the light in the darkness for someone else.

That's what I had in mind when I wrote this post on our Facebook page:

Does anyone know what it's like for a Mother to hear her Daughter say these words, "I'm shooting heroin," "I'm do-ing meth," "We've been speed-balling" or "I haven't slept in 3 days because of a drug binge?" Has anyone experienced the pain of a Mom making eye contact with her Daughter as she walks into a courtroom in orange scrubs while shackled and cuffed? Does anyone understand the pain of a Mother sitting within arm's reach of her Daughter crying in court, guarded by detention officers as she battles her maternal instinct to hug and soothe her Daughter's pain, all while struggling with her own? Has anyone ever experienced the agony of a Grandmother watching her grandsons weep as they try to communicate with their Mother behind a plate of glass? Does anyone know what it's like for a family to try to enjoy a holiday while their Daughter, Mother, Sister, Aunt, Granddaughter sits in a cell?

Has any other Mother experienced the joy of hugging her Daughter, just released from jail, as she runs into your arms? Is there any Mom who has experienced the sinking feeling of dread when she discovers her Daughter has relapsed? Can anyone fathom the feeling of betrayal when a Mom finds out people that she thought she could trust encouraged her Daughter's addictions? Has any parent ever experienced the agony of kicking their precious Daughter out of the house due to a broken sobriety contract? Has any other Mother laid awake at night wondering if her Daughter was alive, dead or being mistreated? Has any parent ever heard the dreaded and horrifying word...deceased? Is there any wife who has witnessed the agonized wails of her husband, the Father of his deceased Daughter? Has any family member mourned the loss of a precious soul, hungering to hold her again?

I have. She's my Daughter and I am her Mother, and my husband is her Father and our children are her siblings, and our Mothers are her Grandmothers, and our siblings are her Aunts and Uncles and our Grandsons are her children. We have, Dear God, we have experienced all of this and more... have you? We pray not. For anyone who may be reading this, stay away from drugs and don't abuse alcohol. PLEASE, don't suffer or let your family suffer as we have.

I would not claim or even pretend that I have become an "expert" on everything that relates to addiction. I'm only an expert on my own personal experience. But based on the journey I have followed as Misty's mother, I do have ideas and suggestions that I'm happy to pass along.

When it comes to defining what addiction is, what causes it, and how best to treat it, there are dozens of professionals out there whose teachings we can learn from. The mental health system certainly opened the door for a more diverse treatment approach when it determined that addiction is a disease and that addicts are pre-disposed to it genetically. My own belief is that addiction is caused by a combination of factors, including genetic background, personal make-up and personality, emotional and psychological wounds and our willingness and ability to deal with them. It's not all one root cause. Addiction really is a health problem, moral problem, emotional problem, psychological problem and genetic problem all rolled into one.

For those like me who carry addiction in our genes, we may be predisposed to it but I believe we can choose what to do with that influence. My siblings and I all inherited the addiction gene from our dad, but we all traveled different paths as it relates to alcoholism. When I first chugged alcohol and could sense the dark hole I could so easily be sucked into, I stopped. Misty may have carried the addiction gene from her grandparents on both sides of her family but so did her five siblings, and none of them are addicts today—thank God! The way I see it, addiction becomes a disease over time by the way it changes you biologically. That's part of what was happening to Misty when the demons took hold. She was truly sick.

I also believe in the value of calling upon multiple approaches in treating addiction. As millions of recovering alcoholics and addicts have discovered, AA and NA can be an extremely valuable resource in providing a structured program to get off booze and drugs and rebuild a healthy life. Still, I don't think AA is for everyone. As a Christian, I trust in the power of faith-based programs such as Celebrate Recovery. Yet I have to admit I have seen successful recoveries without a Christian orientation either. To me, having many different philoso-phies and foundations of treating addiction is a good thing. Addicts and their families can explore what fits best for them. We're all indi-viduals. What's important is to recognize that help is out there...and that any addict *needs* help!

Please bear in mind that the tips or ideas that I am about to share with you come from just one voice in this vast underworld of addiction. They are not meant to be "the right" answers for you or anyone else, and they originate as much from my heart as from my head. I invite you to take what may be useful for you and leave the rest.

Suggestions for Addicts

- **Remember that you have inherent worth.**

If you are wrestling with alcohol or drugs, you probably feel very badly about yourself. To climb out of the abyss, it's vital to understand and believe that you are inherently worthy of love, caring, assistance and a healthy and satisfying life. You are born with this inherent value, and no matter what you have done or what has been done to you, that value remains. Avoid the urge to treat yourself as anything less than an inher-ently valuable human being. When you take that step, you can act on your own behalf and embrace the opportunities in front of you.

- **Surround yourself with healthy people who care about you and your welfare.**

Addicts often are guided by a destructive tendency to only trust and associate with other addicts. That will only perpetuate your continued usage of alcohol and drugs. To break free of the trap, find even one clean and sober person to befriend and learn from. It doesn't have to be a family member. If you attend AA or NA meetings, you will have many options, including your own sponsor. Anyone who has success-fully blazed the trail of recovery can offer you both an understanding of what you're going through and a model for how to move in the right direction.

- **Consider the pain you are causing your family.**

If you have been closely reading the story of Misty and our family, you have seen and heard mountains of evidence of what the fami-lies of addicts endure every day. Do not fool yourself into believing that your destructive behavior is only hurting you. Steer clear of the mistaken assumption that even if something bad happens to you, it's your life and it shouldn't matter to anyone else. The reality is that your addiction is like a giant boulder storming down a hill, and it can crush anyone else in its path. Somewhere inside you do know that those who love you will hurt and continue to hurt while you choose to go on using drugs. Open up to that voice inside and listen...before it's too late.

- **Get help now!**

So many addicts wait and wait until things get "really bad" before they even consider reaching out for assistance. Call it denial, call it stubbornness, call it distorted thinking—it doesn't matter. The longer you wait, the further your disease will progress. And the faster you act, the greater the chances are that you will be able to forge a successful recovery.

The lifelines are there waiting for you, and all you have to do is to execute a quick and easy search online for "addiction recovery" or "help with addiction" to know where to turn to grab hold: AA or NA, Salvation Army programs, treatment centers in your region or far away, a safe distance from local triggers and suppliers, hotlines to contact right in the moment to help you sift through the many options available to you and make a positive first step. YOU CAN DO IT!

Suggestions for the Loved Ones of Addicts

- **Talk about it!**

We all know the importance of educating our children about the dangers of alcohol and drugs while they are growing up. Unfortunately, when a family member does fall into addiction, many families turn silent out of fear, embarrassment, shame or simply confusion about what is right. They don't talk about the problem with the addict, they don't talk about it among themselves, and they try to hide what's happening from those around them. Do not make this mistake. No matter how frustrating it can be, keep an open channel of communication with your loved one hooked on drugs. And talk about the problem with your children, your spouse, your siblings and anyone else who loves the person who is suffering. You all share this struggle, and talking about it will enable everyone to maintain the awareness, the understanding, the compassion and the determination to face the situation in the best possible light. Remember, the addict is prone to lying and manipulation. With a united family, you stand a better chance of deflecting those attempts and summoning the strength and wisdom to help the addict.

The need to talk about addiction extends beyond families. The problems of addiction and the need to work on behalf of addicts is something that should be discussed much more often and more seriously among physicians and mental health professionals, addiction experts, lawmakers, clergy, community leaders and anyone else who may have a hand in enhancing the prospects of recovery for women and men hooked on drugs.

- **Don't keep secrets in your family.**

While this point relates to the need to talk about addiction, it deserves special mention because it's a common problem among the families of addicts. In our family we must humbly admit that there were secrets kept about Misty's alcohol and drug use, and the real impact it was having. Often those secrets were hidden out of the best of intentions, but the reality was that keeping secrets perpetuated the problems and sabotaged the opportunity to make informed decisions. Lots of us knew only pieces of the puzzle; if we had held all of the pieces in our hands we just might have known how to solve that puzzle. From the first sign of trouble with addiction, seek a family commitment to share information and experiences in the name of knowing exactly what is going on and what can be done about it. With addiction, there really can be strength in numbers.

- **Remember that you didn't cause it and you can't cure it.**

Parents especially have to fight the tendency to blame: either for what we did wrong while the addict was growing up, or for all those times when we may have fallen into enabling or made other mistakes while trying to deal with our addicted son or daughter. I had to learn to catch myself when I was tempted to blame our parenting for any childhood wounds Misty suffered under our roof. I had to remind myself that although we certainly weren't the perfect family, Misty never had to see her parents drinking or drugging. She also didn't suffer molestation or violence, as I had while I was growing up. If she was hurt by other things we did, she had the opportunity to explore her pain and pursue healing so that the past would not steer her toward addiction. And when she was caught up in addiction, we had to remember that we could try to support, encourage and point her in the right direction, but the final choice of whether or not to pursue recovery was always Misty's to make. All we can do as parents is to enter fully into each and every moment with the addict and do our best.

- **Avoid feeling guilty when you don't believe the addict.**

Let's face it, addicts mess with your head. They become masters at lying, manipulating, denying, blaming others and otherwise convincing you that things are not what they seem. Still, as parents we shy away from confronting the addict on this behavior and get caught up in *wanting* to believe that what the addict says is true. When Misty was so closely guarding her backpack while living in our house, I *knew* she had drugs in there. But when Misty would casually deny it and turn the tables on me for being suspicious, I backed off instead of demanding that she open the backpack and suffer the consequences of breaking her agreement not to use or keep drugs in our home. If we really want to help the addict that we love, we need to let go of the guilt from not believing our loved one and act on the basis of reality. Keep in mind when you hear the angry denials and attempts to blame you that those words of distortion are coming from the addict, not the person trapped inside. Your job is to make choices on behalf of that person that you love.

- **Get help for yourself.**

Families of addicts can easily get swept up into obsessing and strategizing on the best way to assist the addict. In doing so, we forget the need to get help for ourselves. Dealing with an addict in the family is physically, emotionally, psychologically and spiritually draining. It can literally suck the life right out of you. To maintain your own health and sanity, and to be more available to assist the addict, pursue active steps to take care of yourself. Al-Anon and other support groups are a valuable resource for many, although I found that it didn't click for me because I spent so many hours working with groups in my professional work that I wasn't comfortable listening to others in this setting. Explore your options, which may include these support groups or seeing a therapist, turning to a trusted clergy member, or finding friends and allies who understand what you are facing and can be there with you every step of the way.

- **Understand that when even addicts do make the choice to seek recovery, there is no guarantee of instant and lasting success.**

My friend Roy at Bridges Network tried and failed at recovery eight times before he finally defeated the demons and turned his life around. Relapses happen. They don't mean that your loved one can never get well or has given up, or that *you* should give up. As the families of addicts, we can certainly advise our loved one on choices that may yield the greatest chance of success. I have heard from many professionals that addicts who go far from home for treatment often fare better because they are cut off from their network of addict friends during and after their rehab stay. Other factors can help you find the best fit. However, even what may appear to be the "perfect" recovery program may not take root at first. It may take a second or third attempt before the light bulb finally goes on. Misty's first try left her discouraged and vehement about not going back, but if she had adopted a different attitude and sincerely attempted recovery again and again, I would have been right there with her each and every time. The goal is to keep trying. Even when you make the choice as a parent to let go in actively trying to influence the addict, it doesn't mean that you have given up. It means that you understand that the addict is the one who must decide to change.

For myself, I had to decide that not even Misty's death could make me give up. I have had to keep reminding myself that there is still something I can do to fight addiction. I have to keep telling Misty that, too.

Facebook post, Sept. 27, 2016

Dearest Misty,

I haven't posted here for awhile. I have been more focused on working on your book. However, I know that there are plenty of addicts and their families out there who are hurting and struggling. I feel so relieved that I no longer have to worry that you are being mistreated by corrupt dealers or, for that matter, if you are participating in crimes. I was devastated when I found out you guys had been stealing people's identities, carrying a gun, ski masks and stolen cards. That was like a second death to me. The death of the morality of my Daughter, whom I remember worshipping Jesus, singing to Him on the platform at church, playing the piano, your fingers dancing on the keys. Dear God, what happened to my beautiful, brilliant, intelligent, caring, humorous Daughter? You were my oldest, the one who brightened the room the moment you walked in the door with your laughter and twinkling mischievous eyes. How I miss you, the real Misty, the kind and energetic Misty.

Nothing surprises me anymore, Sweetie. I have learned so much more about the evils of alcohol and drug addiction. I am disgusted by the fact that drinking alcohol is so accepted as a norm in our culture. Dad and I watch the program "Jail" on TV and notice that the commercials that support these shows are often advertising beer and other alcohol products. Don't they realize that the majority of people the police and courts are dealing with are repeat offenders who are most likely alcoholics and addicts? It is so frustrating.

I know that alcohol and drugs possess people until the addict is no longer recognizable to their loved ones. One of the last full sentences I ever uttered to you on the phone was, "Have you lost your friggin' mind????" I'm so glad that the last words you said to me and I said to you during that phone call was, "I love you Mom" and then, "I love you too." I said it with distaste and frustration, but it was said and I meant it

I just couldn't believe you chose to abandon your children, a husband that adored you, your supportive parents, a warm home, food and most of all a family that loved you. But nothing surprises me anymore. Not when it comes to drugs and alcohol. Misty, how I wish you had humbled yourself and continued with your detox and treatment of alcoholism. If you had done so, I have a strong suspicion you would still be here with us today, strong and capable of living a sober life. But, you didn't listen to any of your concerned family members. I feel angry about this Misty, sad and angry.

The real reason I am writing today is to say that I was in tears once again when I arrived in Prescott Valley to spend time with your Sister Janelle. It is incredibly painful to drive the roads you once traveled to come to Wickenburg and back home to PV with your beautiful family, to see landmarks that remind me of you. My chest swells with ache and tears burn my eyes as I drive through Prescott. Every time I see the courthouse I think of you shackled, cuffed and dressed in orange. Each time I pass areas where you lived, or where we sat and ate together, I am reminded of my terrible loss. My eldest child, my beautiful precious Daughter.

It hurts Misty, it really does, and there is nothing I can do about it except to pray and to reach out to struggling addicts, to other moms and other families. I hope when your book is completed, it will shine a light on what substance abuse looks like, how it changes people, how it wears down families and friends, how it hurts. I hope your story will give people strength and hope to change, to embrace sobriety, to win their lives back, to fight back against evil. I pray that people will seek help.

I hope one day I can drive to Prescott and Prescott Valley without this pain in my chest and tears in my eyes. I feel angry about this Misty, so angry and so very sad. I love you oh so much Misty, and I miss you, your hugs and your laughter.

Love,
Mom

I keep listening for new whispers of hope, and I do what I can to amplify them, to try to build a louder and more joyful sound of addicts in larger and larger circles claiming recovery, with their families celebrating their choice to live a healthy and meaningful life. My faith helps to sustain me, as it has through all the challenges I have faced. When the music plays our songs of praise during our Sunday services at The Place in Wickenburg, I do more than sing. I actively sign the words. As I face the front of the church and look high, I am signing to Jesus. I'm not fluent in American Sign Language, but I've studied the book *The Joy of Signing* by Lottie Riekehof and practice as often as I can. I love signing in church because it's a powerful way to worship the Father—with your body, not just your voice. I believe we are meant to entertain the King of Kings. That is one more way that music lifts my spirits. Just as it always did when Misty would play the piano or sing...

Misty's friend Lisa, who is still in prison, recently shared a vision of what she intends to do with her life when she is released and building on her recovery program. I should mention that Lisa loves to sing and has fond memories of entering a music store in Prescott Valley with Misty and watching my daughter sit down at the piano and play and sing to *Gravity* by John Mayer and *All of Me* by John Legend.

"My drive is to reach other women struggling with addiction and to give them the peace that Misty gave me," Lisa explains. She vows that no matter how old she is, where she is in life, and what new challenges she may face, she will open a halfway house that will include music therapy.

Will this wonderful goal be actualized someday? Well, it's difficult to predict the future of any addict striving for recovery, but I believe in miracles. And I especially want to believe in *this* vision knowing the name that Lisa intends to hang on the entrance to this halfway house:

"The House of Musick."

About the Author

CHERYL HUGHES MUSICK was inspired to share her story after the tragic death of her daughter Misty. Musick has chosen to use Misty's story to help reach others in similar circumstances and show them that there is still time to change their lives.

Musick spent her career in mental health. She has worked with patients suffering from eating disorders, trauma, and chemical addiction. Musick is well versed in many therapeutic techniques, including equine-assisted psychotherapy, animal-assisted therapy, ropes courses, art and recreation therapy, and spiritual therapy. She specializes in body image and is Advanced Certified, Equine Assisted Growth and Learning Association (EAGALA).

Musick is a native of southern California, but she moved out to the Sonoran Desert in Arizona in 1988. She spends her free time enjoying the desert landscape, caring for animals, creating art, practicing music, writing, and teaching at the Place Church in Wickenburg, Arizona.

Contact the Author
For addiction support, treatment center referrals, information or to book speaking engagements, please visit my website:
www.houseofmusick.com

Made in the USA
San Bernardino, CA
19 March 2017